Spiritual Warfare

For the first time ever, the true meaning of Spiritual Warfare has been explained!

Pastor Chris Ojigbani

Copyright © 2009 by Pastor Chris Ojigbani

Spiritual Warfare
For the first time ever, the true meaning of Spiritual Warfare has been explained!
by Pastor Chris Ojigbani

Printed in the United States of America

ISBN 978-1-60791-288-0

All rights reserved solely by the author. The author guarantees all contents are original and do not infringe upon the legal rights of any other person or work. No part of this book may be reproduced in any form without the permission of the author.

Unless otherwise indicated, Bible quotations are taken from The King James Version (KJV).

Covenant Singles and Married Ministries
No 2 Admiralty Road, Lekki Phase I
P.O. Box 70351, Victoria Island,
Lagos, Nigeria
Tel: +w234 1 850 5522, +234 802 717 3678
Website: www.singlesandmarried.org

www.xulonpress.com

Dedication

To the Glory of God

Table of Contents

INTRODUCTION xiii

CHAPTER ONE 19
The Meaning Of Spiritual Warfare
What Is Spiritual? *19*
What Is Warfare? *19*
What Is Spiritual Warfare? *20*

CHAPTER TWO 23
The Devil's Weapons Of Warfare
Does The Devil Have Power Over
  A Christian? *23*
The Weapons Of The Devil *26*

CHAPTER THREE 29
Prayer
What Is Prayer? *29*
Is There Anything Like Dangerous Prayer? *30*
Why Many Wrongly Engage In
  Dangerous Prayer *31*

Types Of Prayer *34*
Prayer Is Not Used In Spiritual Warfare *35*
Why Prayer Is Not Used In
  Spiritual Warfare *35*

CHAPTER FOUR **39**
The Weapons Of Our Warfare
What Are The Weapons Of Our Warfare? *40*
Jane's Testimony *47*

CHAPTER FIVE **57**
The Purpose Of Spiritual Warfare
What Is The Purpose Of Spiritual Warfare? *57*
Where Is The Battleground Of Spiritual
  Warfare? *58*
The Objectives Of The Weapons of
  Spiritual Warfare *60*

CHAPTER SIX **73**
The Anatomy Of Spiritual Warfare
We Have Dominion Over All The Earth 73
Whatever A Man Believes Happens 74
What Do We Believe With? 75
The Tool For Guarding Our Hearts 76
Why The Devil Focuses On The Mind 78
Spiritual Warfare Is A Game Of The Mind 78
Decide To Have Your Miracle Now! 79

CHAPTER SEVEN **83**
The Trick Of Dreams
What Is A Dream? *83*
Sources Of Dreams *83*
How The Devil Uses Dreams As Weapon *85*
Does Eating In The Dream Signify
　Spiritual Attack? *88*
Why Do People Eat In The Dream? *89*
How To Know A Dream From The Devil *90*
The Solution To The Trick Of Dreams *91*

CHAPTER EIGHT **95**
The Trick Of Spirit Husband Or Wife
What Is Spirit Husband Or Wife? *95*
Does Spirit Husband Or Wife Exist? *96*
Do Spirits Get Married? *97*
Can A Christian Have An Evil Spirit? *100*
Can A Spirit Indulge In Sex? *101*
Is There Anything Like Spirit Children? *101*
Does Sex In The Dream Signify
　Spiritual Attack? *102*
Why Do Some People Have Sex In
　The Dream? *103*
The Trick Of Spirit Husband/Wife Exposed *104*
The Solution To The Trick Of Spirit
　Husband/Wife *106*
Bukky's Testimony *108*

CHAPTER NINE 111
The Trick Of Curses
What Is A Curse? *111*
The Sources Of Curses *112*
Can The Devil Curse Anyone He Desires? *112*
Can Prayer Break A Curse? *113*
The Origin Of Curses *113*
Why Do Curses Happen? *114*
The Solution To Curses *114*
Can A Christian Operate Under A Curse? *115*
Do Generational Curses Exist In
   Christianity? *116*
Why Some Suffer From Generational Curses *119*
The Solution To Generational Curses *119*
Caroline's Testimony *120*
The Trick of Achieving Righteousness
   By The Law *121*
The Solution To The Trick Of Curses *122*

CHAPTER TEN 125
The Trick Of Non-Forgiveness
What Is Forgiveness? *125*
How A Person Can Lose His
   Righteousness *126*
How the Devil Uses The Trick Of
   Non-Forgiveness *127*
The Purpose Of The Trick of
   Non-Forgiveness *127*
The Solution To The Trick Of
   Non-Forgiveness *129*

The Mystery Of Forgiveness *130*
How To Know If You Have Forgiven Others *132*
Theresa's Testimony *133*

CHAPTER ELEVEN 137
The Trick Of Deliverance
What Is Deliverance? *137*
Who Needs Deliverance? *138*
Who Can Deliver A Person? *138*
How To Get Deliverance *140*
Who Is A Christian? *141*
Does A Christian Need Deliverance? *142*
The Trick Of Deliverance Exposed *143*
Does A Christian Need Deliverance When
  He Commits Sin? *144*
Is There Anything Like Family Deliverance? *146*
Does Prayer Lead To Deliverance? *147*
Does A Person Experiencing Lack Need
  Deliverance? *150*
Phyna's Testimony *152*

CHAPTER TWELVE 155
The Trick Of Sexual Sins
What Is Sexual Sin? *155*
The Implication Of Sexual Sins *156*
The Trick of Sexual Sins Exposed *157*
The Solution To The Trick Of Sexual Sins *159*

CHAPTER THIRTEEN **161**
The Trick Of Testimony
God Wants You To Testify *162*
Testifying Perfects Blessings *163*

CONCLUSION **165**
My Testimony *171*

Introduction

Why do some people who fast and pray suffer so much lack in their lives while some who do not even fast or pray prosper? Why do some Christians experience lack in their lives while some Non-Christians prosper in almost every area of their lives? Why are many Christians not receiving their heart desires on earth?

The answer to these questions is that being a Christian does not guarantee the fulfilment of your heart desires. **Though God wants you to receive all your heart desires on earth, being a Christian does not guarantee it.** What Christianity guarantees is eternal life.

> *For God so loved the world, that he gave his only begotten Son, that whosoever believeth in him should not perish, but have everlasting life.*
> – John 3:16

For you to have everlasting life, you need to become a Christian. **Though eternal life is much more important than any heart desire you can receive on earth, being a Christian does not guarantee you will receive your heart desires.** Becoming a Christian is not the determining factor of receiving your heart desires. For your heart desires to be accomplished on earth, there is another Scriptural principle you must conform to. This principle determines whether a person will receive his heart desires or not.

Anyone, whether a Christian or not, who conforms to the principle receives his heart desires. This explains why we have so many Non-Christians who get married easily, who enjoy their marriages, and who prosper in other areas of their lives. Anybody who conforms to the principle receives his desires. And anyone who does not conform to the principle suffers affliction on earth, whether he is a Christian or not. This also explains why some Christians suffer afflictions in various areas of their lives.

Conforming to the principle is the determining factor of receiving your heart desires on earth. Once you conform to the principle, you receive your heart desires on earth. This principle can be found in the Second Letter of Apostle Paul to the Corinthians.

> *For though we walk in the flesh, we do not war after the flesh.*
> — 2 Corinthians 10:3

The Scripture above says that though we live in the natural, the war we wage is not natural. This Scripture has several implications.

The first implication of the Scripture is that we are engaged in a war. No one in the natural is excluded from this war. That a person is not aware of the war does not exclude him or her from the war. Everyone is involved in the war.

The second implication of the Scripture is that the war is spiritual. The Scripture says that we live in the natural but the war we wage is not natural. If the war is not natural, then it is spiritual.

The third implication is that for you to effectively walk in the flesh, you have to effectively wage spiritual war. For you to succeed in the natural, you have to succeed in your spiritual war. If you want to receive your heart desires in the natural, you have to win your Spiritual Warfare. The spiritual controls the natural. The natural is subject to the spiritual.

Everything that happens in the natural is predetermined by the spiritual. The natural is controlled by the spiritual. The reason you are reading this book, for example, is because it has been predetermined. And if God has truly predetermined that you read this book, then it is for a purpose. My earnest prayer is that the purpose will be fulfilled in your life in Jesus name.

For you to achieve all your desires on earth, you have to win your Spiritual Warfare. **The determinant of receiving your heart desires is your ability to win your Spiritual Warfare**. If someone wants to get married to the kind of person he wants, all he needs to do is to win his Spiritual Warfare. If a married person wins his Spiritual Warfare, he will unfailingly enjoy his marriage. If a separated person wants to reconcile with his spouse, all he needs to do is to win his Spiritual Warfare.

For you to have good health, you have to win your Spiritual Warfare. If you want to prosper financially, then you have to win your Spiritual Warfare. To succeed on earth, you must win your Spiritual Warfare. **In Heaven there is no Spiritual Warfare you are required to win. But on earth, for you to succeed in anything you do, you must win your Spiritual Warfare.** The understanding of Spiritual Warfare and how to wage the war will empower you to receive all your heart desires on earth.

It is unfortunate that most Christians misunderstand the meaning of Spiritual Warfare. This explains why many Christians suffer different afflictions. Very many people do not even know what Spiritual Warfare really means, how much more how to wage the war. Some call it 'warfare prayers' while some call it 'dangerous prayers'.

Please note that Spiritual Warfare is not related to prayers and has nothing to do with prayers. Prayer is very important but has nothing to do with Spiritual Warfare. This is the reason very many pray so much and still do not receive their heart desires. If Spiritual Warfare were about prayers, you probably wouldn't have any of your needs unmet – because I believe you must have prayed very hard. Spiritual Warfare has no relationship with prayers. Your good understanding of what Spiritual Warfare means and how to wage the war will guarantee your receiving all your heart desires.

What you are about to read in this book, you may never have read or heard in your life. This book is designed to teach you what you have not learnt before so that you can achieve what you have not achieved before. For you to achieve a new thing in life, you must learn to do a new thing. If a person continues to do the same old thing, he will continue to get the same old result. For you to achieve a different result in life, you must learn to do a different thing.

In this book, you will learn to do new things. Because you may not have read or heard what is contained in this book, I have used the Bible as my basis of authority. I made Biblical references of every teaching contained in this book.

If you find any teaching in this book without any clear-cut Biblical reference, do not accept it. But if the teachings contained in this book are Scriptural, please accept them, even if it differs from what you used to know. Whenever a person understands a mystery in the Scripture, he is empowered to achieve a new thing in his life.

In this book, I explained the true meaning of Spiritual Warfare and how to win all your spiritual wars. The content of this book has the capacity to enable you receive your heart desires in every area of your life; but as the apostle of marriage, I focused most of my illustrations on marriage. Though most of the illustrations are focused on marriage, you can certainly apply them to other areas of your life. The purpose of this book, therefore, is to enable you receive all your heart desires in every area of your life.

The content of this book has been tested and proven. It works. I have taught the content of this book for several years before putting them to print. The teaching in this book has produced countless amazing testimonies. When you understand the content of this book, then you will have your own amazing testimony in the name of Jesus Christ our saviour.

CHAPTER ONE

The Meaning Of Spiritual Warfare

In this chapter, you will come to know the true meaning of Spiritual Warfare. For better understanding, I will first explain the meaning of the words 'spiritual' and 'warfare' before explaining the meaning of Spiritual Warfare.

What Is Spiritual?

Spiritual means lacking material body, form or substance. It means what you cannot see, touch or feel.

What Is Warfare?

The Greek rendering of warfare is *strateia*, which is derived from *strateuomai*, and it means military service. It is the act of contending or active struggle between competing entities.

What Is Spiritual Warfare?

Spiritual Warfare means an act of active struggle between human beings and evil spirit beings. For better understanding, let's go to the Book of Ephesians.

> *For we **wrestle** not against flesh and blood, but against principalities, against powers, against the rulers of the darkness of this world, against spiritual wickedness in high places.*
>
> – Ephesians 6:12

The word 'wrestle' in the above Scripture denotes an act of active struggle; it means a combat, which means the same thing as warfare. That means we are engaged in warfare. The Scripture also states clearly that the war is not against human beings. The war is not against your father, your mother, your sibling, your uncle, your aunty, your relative, your in-law, your colleague, your friend, or even your enemies. In Spiritual Warfare, anyone who fights against a human being loses the war. Spiritual Warfare is an unseen war we wage against unseen beings. The war is against evil spirit beings, which include principalities, powers, the rulers of the darkness of this world, and spiritual wickedness in high places. **Spiritual Warfare, therefore, is an act of active struggle between human beings and evil spirit beings.**

For a clearer understanding of the subject of Spiritual Warfare, it is very important you know the kind of weapons that are used in the warfare. There is no warfare without weapons. If we are engaged in warfare with the evil spirits, it means that there must be some weapons used by both the human beings and the evil spirits.

Your knowledge of the weapons will enable you know how to wage the war effectively. If a person does not know the weapons, how can he or she successfully wage war against the evil spirits? When a person lacks knowledge of the weapons, he or she cannot effectively wage the war and will end up suffering so many afflictions.

What weapons do the evil spirits use in the war? What weapons do we use in the war?

CHAPTER TWO

The Devil's Weapons Of Warfare

So many people misinterpret the devil's weapon as 'power' and are busy fighting against the power of the devil. The question is: does the devil have power over a Christian? Before showing you the weapons the devil uses in Spiritual Warfare, let us first find out if the devil has power over a Christian.

Does The Devil Have Power Over A Christian?

The devil has no single power over a Christian. Every power of the devil was taken from him when Christ died on the Cross of Calvary. For a clearer understanding, let me take you to the Garden of Eden when God created man. After creation, God gave man more powers than any other creature of His. Man was created to operate like God on earth.

And God said, Let us make man in our image, after our likeness: and let them have dominion over the fish of the sea, and over the fowl of the air, and over the cattle, and over all the earth, and over every creeping thing that creepeth upon the earth.

– Genesis 1:26

God made man to be like Him. Man has the nature and characteristics of God. God also gave man dominion, but He limited man's dominion to earth. **The difference between man and God is that while God has power and dominion over both the heavens and the earth, man's dominion is limited to earth alone.**

After man committed the sin of disobedience in the Garden of Eden, it led to the fall of man. Man lost his power and dominion to the devil. Please take note that the reason man lost his powers to the devil was because he committed sin. The Last Adam, Jesus Christ later came and redeemed us from our sins. If sin was the reason man lost his powers to the devil and Christ has redeemed us from sin, what then happened to the powers? God took back all the powers from the devil.

Many people believe that when man committed sin, he lost his powers to the devil but don't want to accept that when Christ paid for the sins, the powers were taken back from the devil. If you believe that man lost his powers to the devil because he committed sin, then you should believe that when Jesus Christ paid the penalty for the sin, the powers were taken back from the devil. Is there any passage in the Bible that tells us the powers were taken from the devil? Let's go to the Book of Colossians.

And having spoiled principalities and powers, he made a show of them openly, triumphing over them in it.
— Colossians 2:15

The above Scripture tells us that God *spoiled* all principalities and powers when Christ was crucified on the cross. The phrase 'principalities and powers' refers to evil spirits. That means the Scripture is saying that God *spoiled* evil spirits, including the devil. What does the word 'spoil' mean? The Greek rendering of the word 'spoil' is **apekduomai** and it means 'to strip someone of power and authority'.

So what the Scripture means is that God took away power and authority from the evil spirits when Christ died on the Cross of Calvary. When a person gives his life to Christ, the devil will no longer have power over him. Apart from the fact that the devil does not have power and authority over a Christian, every Christian has power and authority over the devil.

> *Then he called his twelve disciples together, and gave them power and authority **over all devils**.*
>
> – Luke 9:1

You have power over all devils. The devil has no single power over a Christian. **Unfortunately many people who are more powerful than the devil are seeking for deliverance. Though they are more powerful than the devil, they are looking for who will deliver them from the same devil. What ignorance!** Some are even trying to defeat the devil without knowing the devil has already been defeated. When Christ died on the Cross of Calvary, not only was the devil defeated, God also stripped him of power and authority.

If the devil has no power over a Christian, how then does he engage in Spiritual Warfare against us? What weapons does the devil use in Spiritual Warfare?

The Weapons Of The Devil

The devil uses only one set of weapons in Spiritual Warfare. And the weapons can be seen in the Bible.

> *Put on the whole armour of God, that ye may be able to stand against the **wiles** of the devil.*
>
> – Ephesians 6:11

We are advised in the above Scripture to use the complete armour of God, which is the complete weapon of war of God. The Scripture also tells us the reason we have to use the armour of God – to be able to withstand the *wiles* of the devil. If we are resisting the *wiles* of the devil, it means that wiles are the weapons of the devil.

In warfare, whatever you are resisting is the weapon of your opponent. If for instance John is asked to use a shield to enable him resist the arrows of Peter, it means that Peter's weapons are arrows. Because Peter is using arrows, John is advised to use a shield to enable him resist the arrows.

Anything you are resisting in warfare is the weapon of your opponent. The Scripture above advises us to use God's armour to enable us resist the *wiles* of the devil. If we are resisting the wiles of the devil, it then means that wiles are the weapons the devil is using against us.

What then is *a wile*? The Greek rendering of the word 'wile' is ***methodeia*** and it literally means trick. *Wile* in English language also means trick.

So the weapons of the devil are tricks. In Spiritual Warfare, we resist the tricks of the devil. There is no other weapon the devil uses in Spiritual Warfare apart from tricks. The devil is very tricky. This explains why some people who fast and pray so much still suffer afflictions. They suffer afflictions because prayer and fasting is not the solution to the tricks of the devil.

The only solution to the tricks of the devil is the whole armour of God and prayer is not part of the armour of God.

This also explains why so many people who misconstrue Spiritual Warfare as 'dangerous prayer' or 'warfare prayer' suffer many afflictions in their lives. Because very many people misunderstand Spiritual Warfare as 'dangerous prayer' or 'warfare prayer', I have deemed it necessary to explain the meaning of prayer and why it does not make any impact in Spiritual Warfare.

CHAPTER THREE

Prayer

What Is Prayer?

Prayer is an act of communication between man and God. Please take note that it is only a communication between man and God that can be referred to as prayer. If a man's communication is not with God, it doesn't mean prayer no matter where or when such communication was made.

And it came to pass, that, as he was praying in a certain place, when he ceased, one of his disciples said unto him, Lord, teach us to pray, as John also taught his disciples.
And he said unto them, When ye pray, say, Our Father which art in heaven.
— Luke 11:1-2

In the Scripture above, Jesus Christ taught us that our prayer must be to our Heavenly Father. Any communication that is not with our Heavenly Father is not prayer. If a man communicates with another man or with a witch or a demon, it does not mean prayer. **For any communication of man to be regarded as prayer, it must be with God. If it is not with God, it is not prayer.**

Is There Anything Like Dangerous Prayer?

In Christianity, there is nothing like 'dangerous prayer' or 'warfare prayer'. Prayer means communication between man and God. Any communication of man that is not with God cannot be regarded as prayer. When a man communicates with another man or with a witch or a demon, it does not mean prayer. In 'dangerous prayer', the communication is not between man and God but between man and another man, witch or demon.

What most people call 'dangerous prayer' is when they issue decree for their enemies to die or for fire to consume their enemies. For example, a man speaking thus "I command any evil arrow against me to go back to sender." Such communication is not with God. The communication is with the sender of the evil arrow, which is a human being. Evil arrows originate from human beings. Though human beings are manipulated by evil spirits to send evil arrows, human beings do the actual sending of evil arrows. So, when a man commands arrows to go back to sender, he is communicating with a fellow human being and not with God. And because such communication is not with God, it is not prayer.

Some engage in 'dangerous prayer' or 'warfare prayer' all night, thinking they are praying, without knowing they are busy communicating with men or witches. And because their communication is not with God, it cannot be regarded as prayer. For any communication of man to be regarded as prayer, it must be with God. If it is not with God, it is not prayer. There is nothing like 'dangerous prayer' in Christianity.

Why Many Wrongly Engage In Dangerous Prayer

(1) One of the major reasons many people engage in 'dangerous prayer' or 'warfare prayer' is because they misinterpret Spiritual Warfare to mean fighting of battles. Because of the term 'warfare', they see it as battle and as such engage in what they call 'dangerous prayer' or 'warfare prayer'. Please note that we don't fight battles in Christianity. Our battles belong to the Lord (2 Chronicles 20:15).

(2) Some who pray 'dangerous prayer' feel there is nothing wrong in it because they believe they are revenging evil acts against them.

But in Christianity, we are not permitted to revenge. The Bible says we should not repay anyone evil for evil.

Recompense to no man evil for evil.
— Romans 12:17

It is very clear from the above Scripture that God does not want us to repay anyone evil for evil. Vengeance does not belong to us. It belongs to the Lord.

Dearly beloved, avenge not yourselves, but rather give place unto wrath: for it is written, Vengeance is mine; I will repay, saith the Lord.
— Romans 12:19

(3) There is another set of Christians who believe they ought to pray 'dangerous prayer' or 'warfare prayer' in order to avoid evil from happening to them. They believe they can use such prayers to deliver themselves from evil. But that is wrong because in Christianity, it is not our responsibility to deliver ourselves from evil. It is God's responsibility to deliver us from every kind of evil.

And it came to pass, that, as he was praying in a certain place, when he ceased, one of

his disciples said unto him, Lord, teach us to pray, as John also taught his disciples.
*And he said unto them, When ye pray, **say, Our Father which art in heaven**, Hallowed be thy name. Thy kingdom come. Thy will be done, as in heaven, so in earth.*
Give us day by day our daily bread.
*And forgive us our sins; for we also forgive every one that is indebted to us. And lead us not into temptation; **but deliver us from evil.***
— Luke 11:1-4

From the above passage, it is very glaring that our prayer must be to Our Father who is in heaven. And part of the prayer request to Our Father is to deliver us from evil. **That means it is God's responsibility to deliver us from mischief, error and all kinds of evil influence. When a man starts delivering himself from evil, there is a problem – a serious problem.**

In Christianity, we don't deliver ourselves from evil. Witches deliver themselves from evil but in Christianity, we have a Father who protects and delivers us from all evil. And guess what? Our Father does the protection better than anyone else. 'Dangerous prayer' does not exist in Christianity. All our battles belong to God.

Types Of Prayer

To enable you know when you are actually praying and when you are not, I consider it necessary to show you the various types of prayers.

Prayer of Worship

Prayer of worship is when a man adores or admires God. It is when a man expresses a feeling of profound love to God.

Prayer of Thanksgiving

This is the kind of prayer in which a man appreciates and gives thanks to God for what He has done for him.

Prayer of Request

This is when a person asks God to grant his need or someone else's need. It can also be called prayer of petition.

Prayer of Repentance

Prayer of repentance is when someone, who is regretful of what he did or what he failed to do, asks God for forgiveness.

Prayer Is Not Used In Spiritual Warfare

Prayer is very important but it is not used in Spiritual Warfare. This explains why many engage in so much 'dangerous prayer' and 'warfare prayer' and still suffer so many afflictions. Prayer is not used in Spiritual Warfare. The essence of prayer is for us to communicate with our Heavenly Father and not for warfare. Let me show you why prayers are not used in Spiritual Warfare.

Why Prayer Is Not Used In Spiritual Warfare

(1) *Spiritual Warfare is not against God*

Prayer means communication with God. That means when a person is talking with God, he is praying. If prayer means talking with God, then it is not used in Spiritual Warfare because the war is not against God. How can talking with God be regarded as warfare when the war is not against God? Prayer can only be used in Spiritual Warfare if the war is against God. But because the war is not against God, talking with God (prayer) cannot be regarded as warfare.

Even if you communicate with God and ask Him to fight for you, the communication (prayer) still cannot be regarded as warfare. Prayer is very important but it's not used in Spiritual Warfare.

(2) *Prayer is not a solution to the tricks of the devil*

Another reason prayer is not used in Spiritual Warfare is that Spiritual Warfare is a war in which we resist the tricks of evil spirits. And prayer is not a solution to the tricks of evil spirits. Prayer does not solve the problem of tricks. The solution to the tricks of the devil is the whole armour of God. Remember the Scripture in Ephesians says we should put on the whole armour of God to enable us resist the tricks of the devil.

*Put on the whole armour of God, that ye may be able to stand against the wiles **(tricks)** of the devil.*
— Ephesians 6:11

The Scripture does not say we should pray to enable us resist the tricks of the devil. It says we should put on the whole armour of God if we want to resist the tricks of the devil. So the solution to the tricks of the devil is to put on the whole amour of God.

The reason many Christians pray very hard and still suffer afflictions is because prayer is not a solution to the tricks of the devil. If prayer were a solution to the tricks of the devil, I am sure that most Christians wouldn't have any problem at all because most Christians pray very well. **The only solution**

to the tricks of the devil is to put on the complete armour of God, which means making use of all the weapons of Spiritual Warfare.

(3) *Prayer is not a weapon of Spiritual Warfare*

There is no place it is said in the Bible that prayer is a weapon of Spiritual Warfare. In the Book of Ephesians, the Bible gives us a list of the complete armour of God and does not include prayer. Because most people wrongly believe that Spiritual Warfare is fought with prayers, they find it difficult to accept that prayer is not a weapon of warfare.

Please take note that I am not criticising prayer. I am not saying you should stop praying. You ought to pray without ceasing. Personally, I pray every time. But I want you to know that because prayer is not a weapon of Spiritual Warfare, it is not used in Spiritual Warfare. I want you to focus on using the right weapons of Spiritual Warfare to wage all your spiritual wars so that you will achieve all your heart desires on earth.

In the next chapter, I will show you all the weapons of Spiritual Warfare. The knowledge of the weapons of Spiritual Warfare will empower you to wage your spiritual wars properly.

CHAPTER FOUR

The Weapons Of Our Warfare

The weapons of our warfare, which also means the armour of God, are what you need to succeed on earth. For you to succeed on earth, you have to succeed in your Spiritual Warfare. And for you to successfully engage in Spiritual Warfare, you have to make use of the weapons of our warfare. So the weapons of our warfare are what you need if you want to succeed on earth.

For a person to get married without further delay, he or she needs to use the weapons of our warfare. When a married person makes use of the weapons of our warfare, he/she enjoys his/her marriage. Even a separated person's marriage is reconciled when he/she makes use of the weapons of our warfare.

To prosper financially, you need to make use of the weapons of our warfare. You also need the weapons of our warfare if you want to have good health. When a sick person makes use of the weapons of our warfare, he becomes well. To succeed in any area of your life, you need to make use of the weapons of our warfare.

When you make use of the weapons of our warfare, you will win all your Spiritual Warfare and you will in turn receive all your heart desires on earth. If making use of the weapons of our warfare enables a person to receive his desires on earth, then it is very important you have knowledge of the weapons and how to make use of them.

What Are The Weapons Of Our Warfare?

Apostle Paul in his Letter to the Ephesians listed all the weapons of our warfare.

*Wherefore take unto you **the whole armour of God**, that you may be able to withstand in the evil day, and having done all, to stand.*
Stand therefore, having your loins girt about with truth, and having on the breastplate of righteousness;
And your feet shod with the preparation of the gospel of peace;
Above all, taking the shield of faith, wherewith ye shall be able to quench all the fiery darts of the wicked.
And take the helmet of salvation, and the sword of the Spirit, which is the word of God.
– Ephesians 6:13-17

Before listing the armour of God, Apostle Paul first called it *the whole armour,* which means the complete armour. What that means is that the list of armour he gave us is the complete list. It also means that any item not mentioned in the list is not part of the armour of God. No matter how important you feel such item is, if it is not among the complete armour of God, then it is not part of the armour of God.

Apostle Paul also did another interesting thing in listing the complete armour. He likened all the armour of God he listed to the physical armour of a Roman soldier. He did this to enable us have good understanding of the armour of God and their functions. For example he likened salvation to helmet. What that means is that the function a helmet has in the life of a Roman soldier in physical warfare is the same function salvation has in our lives in Spiritual Warfare. All the armour of God he listed, he likened to physical armour. So any item he didn't liken to physical armour is not part of the armour of God.

Knowledge of the complete armour of God will enable you succeed in Spiritual Warfare which will in turn empower you to receive all your heart desires. Let us examine the complete armour of God in detail.

(1) *Truth*

> *Stand therefore, having your loins girt about with* **truth**.
> – Ephesians 6:14

The first armour of God Apostle Paul talked about is **truth.** He likened it to the belt a Roman soldier puts around his loins (waist). No soldier is complete without a belt. The function a belt has in the life of a Roman soldier in physical warfare is the same function **truth** has in our lives in Spiritual Warfare.

What then is *truth*? The Greek rendering of the word *truth* is *aletheuo* and it means to speak the truth. What that means is that for you to win spiritual war, you must speak the truth always. Anything you will do that will put you in a position to tell lies, don't do it. In Christianity, we are not permitted to tell lies. Lies belong to the devil.

Ye are of your father the devil, and the lusts of your father ye will do. He was a murderer from the beginning, and abode not in the truth, because there is no truth in him. When he speaketh a lie, he speaketh of his own; for he is a liar, and the father of it.

– John 8:44

Every liar belongs to the devil because the devil is the father of all lies. **If you want to succeed in Spiritual Warfare, you must avoid telling lies. From now onwards, ensure you speak the truth at all times.**

(2) Righteousness

The second armour is **righteousness.**

... and having on the breastplate of righteousness.
- Ephesians 6:14

Apostle Paul likened righteousness to the physical armour called breastplate. A breastplate is a metallic plate that is worn like a suit, which protects the chest and the stomach. The same way a breastplate protects a Roman soldier in physical warfare is how righteousness protects us in Spiritual Warfare.

Righteousness, which is *dikaiosune* in Greek language, can be defined as a state where no sin is imputed against a person. No one can achieve such a state by works of the law.

Because of the sin of Adam, everybody became sinners. And Jesus Christ, the Last Adam came to redeem us from sin. He lived on earth without sin. His obedience was complete. And on the Cross of Calvary, there was a divine exchange. Jesus took the form of our disobedience and gave us his complete obedience, which made us righteous.

For as by one man's disobedience many were made sinners, so by the obedience of one shall many be made righteous.
– Romans 5:19

So anyone who confesses and believes that God raised Christ from the dead becomes righteous (Romans 10:9). The reason we are righteous is not because we have done anything to deserve it; it is because the obedience of Christ has made us righteous. Righteousness is a gift – it is a free gift (Romans 5:18).

Please take note that being righteous is not enough for you to be protected by the armour of righteousness. For you to be protected by the armour of righteousness, you have to be righteous and also be conscious of the fact that you are righteous. When a person is not aware he is righteous, he suffers like an unrighteous person. This explains why the Bible says that what sets a person free is not truth but knowledge of the truth (John 8:32).

To win your Spiritual Warfare, you must realise that you have a free gift of righteousness. You must know that you are not seeking to be righteous. Knowing that you are righteous is a strong weapon of our warfare.

(3) *The Gospel of Peace*

The third armour of God on the list is the **gospel of peace**

And your feet shod with the preparation of
the gospel of peace.
– Ephesians 6:15

In the Scripture above, Apostle Paul likened the spiritual armour of the gospel of peace to the physical armour of a Roman soldier's boot. What a pair of boots does in the life of a Roman soldier in physical warfare is what the gospel of peace does in our lives in Spiritual Warfare.

What is the gospel of peace? The Greek rendering of the word 'peace' is *eirene* and it means *to join*; *to reconcile*; *to harmonise*; *to live in peace*. The Scripture admonishes us to live in peace with everyone if it depends on us.

If it be possible, as much as lieth in you, live peaceably with all men.
– Romans 12:18

God wants you to live in peace with everyone. **It is amazing that one of the weapons of our warfare is peace. What a contrast! Using peace as a weapon of war. In other words, if you want to win your Spiritual Warfare, you must live in peace with everyone in the physical.** You have to reconcile with everyone if you want to win all your Spiritual Warfare.

Before any Spiritual attack can take place on earth, it must first be approved in the heavens. And before any spiritual attack can be approved in the heavens, there must be a reason. God is fully in charge of everything happening on earth. No one has the right to attack a person without a reason.

Spiritual Warfare

For any spiritual attack to happen, there must be a reason. If there is no reason, no evil can happen to a person. This explains why the Bible says a causeless curse cannot stand (Proverbs 26:2). No spiritual attack can happen without a reason. When a person is living in peace with everyone, then there is no reason to attack such person. On the other hand, when a person contravenes the gospel of peace, it is enough reason for the person to be attacked spiritually.

If you are living in peace with everyone, you cannot be attacked. For a person to be attacked spiritually, he or she would have contravened the gospel of peace. This is the reason the devil or any of his agents manipulate people to contravene the gospel of peace before attacking them.

For instance, if a house-help who is a witch wants to attack her mistress spiritually, she has to first manipulate her to contravene the gospel of peace. The house-help may, for example, deliberately break some expensive plates. And her unsuspecting mistress will become furious and may even beat up the house-help. The moment the mistress is beating the house-help; she is being attacked spiritually because she has contravened the gospel of peace.

But if after the house-help breaks some plates, and the mistress rather than beating the house-help, shows love to her. Then, the mistress has defeated the witch. Whenever you show love to an enemy, you have defeated the person completely. If you show love to your enemy, you have heaped coals of fire on his head (Romans 12:20).

God wants us to live in peace with everyone. It is unfortunate that some people rather than living in peace, are quarrelling and using what they call 'dangerous prayers' against others. If you want to win your spiritual wars, then ensure you live in peace with everyone.

Do you know that when you are not quarrelling with anyone, there is nobody you will pray against? A clear conscience fears no accusation. If you are not quarrelling with anyone, you cannot be afraid of anyone. *Perfect love casts away fear* (1 John 4:18).

Don't focus on who is at fault. Reconcile with everyone, whether you are at fault or not. If you attempt reconciling and the person refuses, then it is no longer dependent on you. In Spiritual Warfare, we are expected to live in peace with everyone and not quarrel or pray against people. Beloved, it is better to live in peace with people than quarrelling. I have seen so many people who reconciled with their enemies record amazing testimonies.

Jane's Testimony

A sister, Jane (not her real name), came to our office for counselling in June 2008 and had an amazing testimony. She had been impregnated by a man and had given birth to a child in 1998. After she had given birth, the father of the child abandoned her and the child. She completely lost contact with him. In a bid to have the father of her child take care of the child, and possibly get married to her, she went to various places for prayer and deliverance. In spite of the various prayer and deliverance sessions, she had no contact with the man.

Ten years later, she heard about our ministry and came for a counselling session. After the counselling session with me, she decided to forgive everyone who sinned against her. She also reconciled with all her enemies and began to pray for them. Two days after the counselling session with me, the father of her son called her, apologised, and proposed marriage to her. Another man also proposed marriage to her but she chose the father of her son.

The following Sunday, her son was reciting a poem in church when a man saw him and gave him a scholarship. What an amazing testimony! She had suffered for the past ten years, taking care of her son single-handedly. But when she practised the gospel of peace by reconciling with her enemies, not only did the father of her son turn up to marry her and take care of her son, her son was also given a scholarship.

It is amazing! **If you want to win your Spiritual Warfare, then you must reconcile and live in peace with everyone. Reconcile with everyone, whether you are at fault or not.** It is a major weapon of Spiritual Warfare.

(4) Faith

> **Above all, taking the shield of faith, wherewith ye shall be able to quench all the fiery darts of the wicked**
> – Ephesians 6:16

The fourth armour of God Apostle Paul explained to us is **Faith**. This armour is the most important armour in Spiritual Warfare. Apostle Paul started the verse by using the term *above all*. *Above all* means most importantly. Faith is the most important weapon of Spiritual Warfare. He likened it to a *shield* which is a physical armour used by Roman soldiers. A shield is a protective covering made of iron. It is used to intercept arrows. The same function a shield has in the life of a Roman soldier in physical war is the same function faith has in our lives in Spiritual Warfare.

Apostle Paul went further to explain that faith is what quenches the fiery darts of the wicked. The fiery darts of the wicked mean evil arrows. So faith is what we use to quench evil arrows. What that means is that if you want to quench evil arrows, what you need to make use of is faith. It also implies that prayer does not quench evil arrows. If prayer quenches evil arrows, the Bible would have said that *faith and prayer* quench evil arrows. But the Scripture says *faith, wherewith ye shall be able to quench all the fiery darts of the wicked.* **It means that only faith quenches evil arrows.**

Another interesting thing is that the Bible says it quenches ***all** the fiery darts of the wicked*. That means faith quenches all evil arrows and not some. **If faith quenches all evil arrows, which arrow would prayer quench?** Only faith can quench evil arrows.

What is faith? Faith is called *pistis* in Greek language and it means to believe. By believing no evil arrow can touch you, then no evil arrow can touch you. When a person believes an evil arrow would touch him, whether he prays or not, he would be affected by the evil arrow because prayer does not stop evil arrows. **In life, you get what you believe and not what you pray for.**

When a person sends an evil arrow back to the sender, it is an indication he believes that an evil arrow would touch him and therefore attempts to send it back. If he believes an evil arrow cannot touch him, he wouldn't attempt to send it back. So when a person sends an evil arrow back to the sender, it is an affirmation that he believes it would touch him. And for that reason the evil arrow would affect him because whatsoever a person believes happens to him.

Though he prayed against the evil arrow, it would still affect him because prayer does not stop evil arrows. It is what a person believes that happens to him, whether he prays or not. If you don't want an

Spiritual Warfare

evil arrow to affect you, then you must believe that no evil arrow can touch you. And in that case you don't have to send an evil arrow back to the sender because you are sure it cannot touch you.

Once you are sure an evil arrow cannot touch you, then it cannot touch you. This explains why a Non-Christian who is not diabolic would say no evil arrow can touch him and no evil arrow touches him. Because such person believes no evil arrow can touch him, if all the witches and occultists in the world come together to attack him, they cannot harm him. If you believe an evil arrow cannot touch you, it would not touch you. If an evil arrow does not affect a Non-Christian because he believes it cannot touch him, how much more a Christian?

Several years ago, I used to make a wrong declaration. I would always say: "I break and destroy the hold of witchcraft power over my life." Then one day, after making such declaration, I asked myself if there was any hold of witchcraft power over my life. It then dawned on me that there was no witchcraft power over my life because witchcraft cannot affect a true Christian. That was how I became free from such ignorance. And from that day I never bothered myself about breaking any witchcraft power over my life because I am very sure there is no witchcraft power over my life.

I challenge you to exercise your faith and believe that no evil arrow can touch you. Faith is the only weapon that quenches evil arrows. If you have been sending evil arrows back to sender, stop, because they cannot touch you. Exercise your faith now.

(5)　*Salvation*

> *And take the helmet of **salvation**.*
> *– Ephesians 6:17*

The next armour of God is **salvation**. Apostle Paul likened the armour of salvation to the physical armour of helmet. What helmet does in the life of a Roman soldier in physical warfare is what salvation does in our lives in Spiritual Warfare. Salvation is what protects our head in Spiritual Warfare. This armour is very important because the head is one of the most vital parts of man.

Salvation, which is *soterion* in Greek language, means to save or to deliver. Salvation comes only from Christ. When a person confesses and believes that God raised Christ from the dead, he receives salvation (Romans 10:9). If you have confessed and believed God raised Christ from the dead, then you are already saved.

(6)　*The Word of God*

> *... and the sword of the Spirit, which is the **word of God**.*
> *- Ephesians 6:17*

The last armour is the **Word of God**. Apostle Paul likened it to a sword. The function of a sword in the life of a Roman soldier in physical warfare is the same function the Word of God has in our lives in Spiritual Warfare. It is the only offensive weapon we have in Spiritual Warfare. The first five explained above are defensive weapons; they are protective weapons. They actually protect a person from head to toe. The Word of God is the only offensive weapon of Spiritual Warfare.

The Word of God in the passage above is ***rhema*** in Greek language and it means *an utterance* of God. It is a verse or a passage of the Scripture that the Holy Spirit reveals specifically to a person for a specific situation.

If you want *rhema*, you have to study your Bible always. Ensure you study your Bible everyday. Don't read the Bible as a novel; prayerfully study it. It doesn't make sense that you read so many chapters and yet receive no revelation. It is better you study a few verses of the Scripture and receive revelation than for you to read several chapters without any revelation.

Several years ago, I got a revelation from the Holy Spirit while studying the First Letter of John. And the revelation changed my life forever.

We know that anyone born of God does not continue to sin; the one who was born of God *keeps him safe, and **the evil one cannot harm him.***

– 1 John 5:18, NIV

When I read the passage above, I got a revelation that the devil cannot harm me. ***Cannot*** in the above passage means that it is impossible for the devil to harm me. I also understood that all I needed to do was to keep myself from sin and the devil cannot harm me. And if I mistakenly sin, I ask God for forgiveness. Since then, I no longer bother myself about fighting the devil because I am very sure the devil cannot harm me.

Seek for *rhema*. And any day you receive a *rhema*, don't let go of it. Always meditate on it. It is the only offensive armour of God.

The Word of God completes the list of the armour of God. In the following two verses (verses 18 and 19), Apostle Paul gave the Ephesians three prayer points. He said they should pray in the Spirit, pray for all saints and pray that utterance should be given to him. Praying in the Spirit, praying for the saints, or praying for Apostle Paul is good but cannot be regarded as armour of God because they weren't likened to physical armour. The prayer points are not part of the armour of God. Besides, how can praying for Apostle Paul to have utterance be regarded as a weapon of our warfare?

Prayer is very important but is not a weapon of Spiritual Warfare. Prayer was not given to us to fight warfare. The essence of prayer is for us to communicate with our Heavenly Father. But to engage in Spiritual Warfare, the weapons we use are the armour of God.

The whole armour is truth, righteousness, the gospel of peace, faith, salvation, and the Word of God. And for Apostle Paul to call them *the whole armour* means they are the complete armour. That means there is no other weapon of Spiritual Warfare (armour of God) that exists besides truth, righteousness, the gospel of peace, faith, salvation, and the Word of God.

Now, we have seen the weapons the devil use in Spiritual Warfare and we have also seen the weapons we use. What is the war all about? What is the purpose of the war? How does the devil make use of his weapons? How do we make use of our weapons? Where does the war take place? To see answers to these questions, come with me to the next chapter.

CHAPTER FIVE

The Purpose Of Spiritual Warfare

What Is The Purpose Of Spiritual Warfare?

In Spiritual Warfare, there is one purpose. **Human beings and evil spirit beings contend for the control of human minds. The devil attempts to corrupt our minds with his tricks while we resist the tricks of the devil with the whole armour of God.**

> *But I fear, lest by any means, as the serpent beguiled Eve through subtilty, so your minds should be corrupted from the simplicity that is in Christ.*
> – 2 Corinthians 11:3

In the above passage, Apostle Paul expresses fear that the devil would corrupt the minds of the Corinthians like he deceived Eve. He also said that the devil deceived Eve through subtlety. Subtlety means tricks. So what the devil used against Eve was not his power but tricks. The devil has not changed. He still uses tricks. The reason the devil used tricks on Eve was that Eve was more powerful than him. After the fall of man, man lost his powers. But when Christ redeemed man from sin by His death on the Cross of Calvary, God stripped the devil of the powers (Colossians 2:15). And anyone who gives his life to Christ becomes more powerful than the devil (Luke 9:1).

Because we are now more powerful than the devil, he uses tricks against us. The devil attempts to corrupt our minds with his tricks and we use the whole armour of God to resist his tricks. It is a contention for the control of our minds. **Spiritual Warfare in Christianity can be defined as a war where we use the armour of God to resist the devils' tricks from corrupting our minds. It is a game of the mind.**

Where Is The Battleground Of Spiritual Warfare?

The mind is the battleground of all Spiritual Warfare. No one has ever seen the devil physically to wage a war against him. The war takes place in

Spiritual Warfare

the mind. When a person loses a war in his mind, it will manifest negatively in his life. But if you win a war in your mind, it will manifest positively in your life. The war takes place in the mind.

It is Spiritual Warfare and not physical. Spiritual means lacking material body, form or substance. It means what you cannot see, touch or feel. If you can see anything, then it is no longer spiritual. For example anointing oil is not spiritual because you can see and even touch it. Spiritual means what you cannot see.

No one has ever seen the mind. No one knows where the mind is located. Everyone agrees that the mind exits but no one has ever seen it. Scientists have been spending millions of dollars looking for the location of the mind but no one has ever found it. **The mind is not seen and the things that are not seen control the things that are seen. The invisible controls the visible. The mind is invisible and Spiritual Warfare takes place in the mind.**

This explains why a person may no longer see the light of the gospel of Christ if the devil blinds his mind.

*In whom the god of this world hath **blinded the minds** of them which believe not, lest the light of the glorious gospel of Christ, who is the image of God, should shine unto them.*
— 2 Corinthians 4:4

To better understand that the mind is the battleground of Spiritual Warfare, let me show you the objectives of the weapons of our warfare from the Scripture. Your understanding of the objectives of the weapons of our warfare will help you know everything about Spiritual Warfare.

The Objectives Of The Weapons Of Spiritual Warfare

The objectives of the weapons of Spiritual Warfare can be seen in the Second Letter of Apostle Paul to the Corinthians.

For the weapons of our warfare are not carnal, but mighty through God to the pulling down of strong holds;
Casting down imaginations, and every high thing that exalteth itself against the knowledge of God, and bringing into captivity every thought to the obedience of Christ.
— 2 Corinthians 10:4-5

The Scripture above started by saying the weapons we use in Spiritual Warfare are not natural. If the weapons are not natural, then they are spiritual. It means that the weapons cannot be seen. Remember the weapons: truth, righteousness, the gospel of peace, faith, salvation, and the Word of God. The passage not only tells us that the weapons are spiritual but also tells us that they are mighty weapons. Though the weapons look ordinary, they are powerful weapons.

The passage above also tells us something else. It tells us what the weapons of Spiritual Warfare are used for, i.e. the objectives of the weapons of our warfare.

(1) Pulling Down of Strongholds

The first objective of the weapons of our warfare, the Bible tells us, is to pull down strongholds. The passage says *the weapons of our warfare are not carnal, but mighty through God to the pulling down of strong holds.* The passage means that the weapons of our warfare are not natural weapons but mighty weapons that are used in pulling down of strongholds. The implication of the passage is that for you to pull down strongholds, you need to use the weapons of our warfare. It also implies that prayer does not pull down strongholds. Only the weapons of our warfare can pull down strongholds and prayer is not one of the weapons of our warfare.

What does 'stronghold' in Spiritual Warfare mean? **It is a wrong firm conviction the devil puts in people's minds to turn down the true Word of God and prevent them from receiving their blessings.** A stronghold is formed by a wrong firm conviction in a person's mind. When a person has a wrong firm conviction in his mind, it forms a stronghold and that wrong conviction will begin to manifest in his life.

For instance, if a 25 years old sister named Esther was told that no female could get married in her family until age 40 because of a curse on her grandfather. And Esther meditated on the issue and realised that none of her elder sisters got married before 40 years of age. For that reason she became convinced that no one in her family could get married before 40 years. Because of Esther's wrong conviction that no female could get married in her family before age 40, it formed a stronghold in her mind. And as a result of that, she would never get married before she turns 40.

No matter the kind of fasting and prayer Esther would do, she cannot get married before 40 years because a stronghold has already been formed in her mind. The only means by which she can get married before age 40 is when the stronghold is pulled down. And the Scripture above says that you can only pull down strongholds by the weapons of our warfare.

What does pulling down of strongholds mean? It means when a wrong firm conviction in a person's mind changes to the right firm conviction. If a wrong firm conviction in a person's mind changes to the right one, then the stronghold in his life has been pulled down. In the case of Esther, if she realises and believes she can get married before age 40, then the stronghold is pulled down. And she will easily get married before she is 40.

Spiritual Warfare

How can the weapons of our warfare (truth, righteousness, the gospel of peace, faith, salvation, and the Word of God) pull down the stronghold in Esther and enable her get married before age 40? When Esther is living in **peace** with everyone, she will no longer be afraid of anyone because perfect love casts away fear (1 John 4:18). **Truth, righteousness** and **salvation** will give her the assurance she is a true child of God. It would also make her believe she is protected by God and would remove fear from her. The **Word of God** will make her know that Christ had redeemed her from curses. And the most important weapon, **faith** would make her believe that she had already been redeemed from curses and for that reason can get married before age 40. Then she would easily get married because whatever a person believes is what happens in his life.

Please take note that every miracle of God is cheap. If it is not cheap, it is not from God. The reason many people struggle in their lives is because they don't use the armour of God. People have afflictions mainly because of the strongholds in their minds. And once you use the armour of God, every stronghold in your mind will be pulled down and you will receive your heart desires effortlessly.

As long as Esther has a firm conviction that a curse against her grandfather prevents the females in her family from getting married before age 40, she will never get married before age 40. Though she may be prayerful, it wouldn't help her pull down the stronghold because strongholds are formed in the mind. And prayer cannot remove what is on a person's mind. No matter how hard Esther would pray, she would still be thinking of the curse against her grandfather.

In fact most of her prayers would be focused on breaking the curse against her grandfather. And the prayer of Esther against the curse on her grandfather is an indication she believes there is a curse on her grandfather that is affecting her. And since she believes there is a curse affecting her, it affects her because whatever a person believes happens in his or her life. **So the more she prays against the curse, the deeper she goes into the problem.**

It is important for you to note that the reason Esther wouldn't get married before 40 years is not that the curse is working in her life but because she believes the curse is working in her life. **It is what you believe that happens in your life and not what you pray for.**

It is also important for you to know that curses cannot work in the life of a Christian. The devil uses the trick of curse to make some Christians believe that Christ did not redeem us from curses, and such Christians attempt to free themselves from curses. It is one of the tricks the devil uses in Spiritual Warfare. In subsequent chapters, I will expose some of the tricks of the devil, including the trick of curses.

(2) Casting Down Imaginations

The second objective of the weapons of our warfare, the Bible tells us is to cast down imaginations.

For the weapons of our warfare are not carnal, but mighty through God to the pulling down of strong holds;
Casting down imaginations, and every high thing that exalteth itself against the knowledge of God, *and bringing into captivity every thought to the obedience of Christ.*
– 2 Corinthians 10:4-5

The first objective of the weapons of our warfare is to pull down strongholds, and we saw that strongholds are **formed in the mind**. And the second objective is to cast down imaginations. Where does imagination take place? The mind. Imagination **takes place in the mind**. Spiritual Warfare is a game of the mind. The Scripture above says that we use the weapons of our warfare to cast down every imagination in our minds that exalts itself against the knowledge of God. The knowledge of God is the Scripture. So it means that we use the weapons of our warfare to cast down every imagination in our minds that is contrary to the Scripture.

For a better understanding of how we use the weapons of our warfare to cast down imaginations,

I will illustrate with Esther again. If a man who proposed marriage to Esther disappointed her. And later, a second man proposed marriage to Esther. If she began to imagine in her mind if the man would disappoint her like the previous man, then the man would disappoint her because that was her imagination. Whatever a person imagines is what happens to him or her.

The power of imagination is very strong. Every physical manifestation in your life is the exact replica of the imagination in your mind. Your imagination forms an image of what will manifest in your life. And the manifestation cannot differ from the image. It is whatever image you form in your mind that manifests. Whether the image is right or wrong, it must manifest exactly as it is in your mind.

A typical illustration of how images manifest is the process of developing a picture taken with an analogue camera. After taking a picture with an analogue camera, what comes out is the negative of the picture, which is also the image of the picture. The image will then be processed and converted to the standard picture. After the processing, whatever is in the image is what will come out as the standard picture. If the image is blurred, then the standard picture must be blurred. If the image does not show the legs of the person, then the standard picture cannot show the legs as well. The standard picture cannot differ from the image; it is the exact replica of the image.

The imagination in your mind forms the image of what will manifest in your life. If someone who is looking for a good job imagines disappointment, then the person will be disappointed. And any day he stops imagining disappointment and starts imagining being employed in a good establishment, then he will unfailingly be employed in a good establishment.

In the case of Esther, if a third man proposes marriage to her, she would still be disappointed if she continues to imagine disappointment. There would then be a pattern; the men would leave Esther in the same manner. If the first man disappointed her after she introduced him to her family, anytime she introduces a would-be spouse to her family, she would start imagining the man would disappoint her like the previous one. And because of such imagination, the man would disappoint her.

Esther would continue experiencing disappointment as long as she continues imagining disappointment. Even when she does not tell anybody she has a marriage proposal, she would still experience disappointment because the cause of the disappointment is the stronghold in her mind. No matter how hard Esther fasts and prays, she would continue to experience disappointments if she continues imagining disappointment. **Whatever you imagine is what happens in your life.**

The only means by which Esther can ever get married is when she casts down such imaginations.

What does the Bible mean by casting down imaginations? It means when a person stops imagining a negative outcome and starts imagining a positive outcome. In the case of Esther, casting down imaginations would mean when she stops imagining disappointment and starts imagining marriage. When she starts imagining her wedding with her fiancé taking place and imagining herself living together with him as a couple, then her marriage would unfailingly take place.

When a person imagines failure and affliction, the person gets failure and affliction whether he prays or not. Prayer does not cast down imaginations. This explains why some people who don't pray, who have never fasted before and who are not diabolic get good jobs, marry without delay and even enjoy their marriages. Once their imaginations are not wrong, they prosper in their lives. They may not make heaven if they die as unbelievers, but they would live well on earth because they don't have wrong imaginations in their minds.

As long as Esther imagines disappointment, she would continue to experience disappointment. Please note that the reason Esther experiences disappointment is not because a witch is attacking her but because of her imagination. The moment she starts imagining marriage, she will then get married without delay. I have seen countless people record amazing testimonies in their lives after casting down wrong imaginations. Most of the people who record such testimonies have actually been going to several places for prayer and deliverance but didn't receive their desires. And few days after I taught them to change their wrong imaginations, they received their desires.

No matter how prayerful a Christian may be, if his imagination is wrong, the wrong things will manifest in his life. Prayer is very good, but does not cast down imaginations. The Bible says that for you to cast down wrong imaginations, you must use the weapons of our warfare.

(3) *Bring into Captivity Every Thought*

The third objective of the weapons of our warfare is to bring into captivity every thought to the obedience of Christ.

> *For the weapons of our warfare are not carnal, but mighty through God to the pulling down of strong holds;*
> *Casting down imaginations, and every high thing that exalteth itself against the knowledge of God,* **and bringing into captivity every thought to the obedience of Christ.**
> – 2 Corinthians 10:4-5

The first objective of the weapons of our warfare is to pull down strongholds and the second objective is to cast down imaginations. And we saw that they take place in the mind. The third objective, in the passage above, is to bring into captivity every thought. Where do thoughts take place? Thoughts take place in the mind. Spiritual Warfare is a game of the mind. **If the three objectives of the weapons of our warfare take place in the mind, then there is no argument that Spiritual Warfare is a game of the mind.**

What does *bringing into captivity every thought to the obedience of Christ* mean? The obedience of Christ is the obedience of the Word of God because Jesus Christ is the Word. So what the Scripture means is that we use the weapons of our warfare to make every thought in our minds to be in accordance with the Word of God.

God recognises the fact that wrong thoughts can come into a person's mind. The devil is the architect of wrong thoughts. He can make anyone think anything. He has the right to inject thoughts into anyone. Remember he injected thoughts into the mind of Jesus Christ when he tempted Jesus. He also injected thoughts into the mind of Eve before the fall of man. He can inject thoughts into anybody's mind.

So, what the passage is saying is that when wrong thoughts come into our minds, we should subject them to be in accordance with the Scripture. We should do the same thing Jesus Christ did when the devil injected thoughts into His mind.

If for example, a man who promised to marry Esther disappointed her and she later meets another man who proposed marriage to her. It is not unusual for the devil to inject thoughts of disappointment into her mind to make her think of disappointment so that she would be disappointed. When thoughts of disappointment come to Esther, she should for example subject her thoughts to the Scripture that says *affliction shall not arise a second time* (Nahum 1:9).

God wants your thoughts to be proper. Why is it necessary for you to ensure that your thoughts are proper? **The reason is that what your thoughts dwell on happens in your life.** This explains why the Bible says that as a man thinks, so is he (Proverbs 23:7).

The Scripture does not say that as you are, so you think. It says that as you think, so you are. In other words, you are what you think; you are your thoughts. It means that every blessing you can ever receive in life is determined by your thoughts. It also means that what you have achieved in your life so far has been determined by your thoughts.

No man or woman is the cause of any affliction you face. Change your thoughts and affliction will be no more in your life. And for your thoughts to change, you have to use the weapons of our warfare.

By now, I believe you have no doubt that all Spiritual Warfare takes place in the mind. The questions now are: Why does Spiritual Warfare take place in the mind? Why is the devil interested in our minds? Why does the devil corrupt our minds with his tricks? In the next chapter, I will treat these and other things you should know regarding Spiritual Warfare.

CHAPTER SIX

The Anatomy Of Spiritual Warfare

—⚏—

We Have Dominion Over All The Earth

You have dominion over all the earth. God gave man more powers than any creature of His. **No one has power over you apart from you.** No limit has been given to man. God gave us dominion over all the earth.

> *And God said, Let us make man in our image, after our likeness: and let them have dominion over the fish of the sea, and over the fowl of the air, and over the cattle, and over all the earth, and over every creeping thing that creepeth upon the earth.*
> — Genesis 1:26

As far as this earth is concerned, we are in charge. You have the right to dominate all the earth. In heaven, you cannot exercise any dominion. Your dominion is limited to the earth.

The heaven, even the heavens, are the LORD's: but the earth hath he given to the children of men.

– Psalm 115:16

We have the power to dominate everything on earth. As far as this earth is concerned, we are gods (John 10:34).

Whatever A Man Believes Happens

Whatever a man believes must happen. **No power is strong enough to stop what a man believes from happening. Anything a man believes must happen: whether such thing is good or bad.** Even God does not stop what we believe from happening because He is the one that gave us the power. Though our saviour and master, Jesus Christ, had the maximum power of God when he was on earth, yet there were some things he couldn't do. The Bible records that He couldn't do mighty works in his village because of their unbelief.

And they were offended in him. But Jesus said unto them, A prophet is not without

honor, save in his own country, and in his own house.
*And he did not many mighty works there because of their **unbelief**.*
— Matthew 13:57-58

In spite of the maximum power of God Jesus Christ had on earth, he was not able to do mighty works in his village because they didn't believe him. In Mark's account, the Bible says Jesus Christ *could not* do mighty works in his village (Mark 6:4-6). The phrase *could not* means that He tried to do mighty works but couldn't. The people needed miracles but Jesus couldn't do mighty works there because they didn't believe that the 'carpenter's son' could do mighty works.

If Jesus Christ couldn't force the people in his village to receive miracles against their belief, then no other power can stop what you believe from happening. Anything you believe must happen.

What Do We Believe With?

If anything we believe happens, then it is important to know what we believe with. We believe with the heart (Romans 10:10). Anything that enters the heart of a person, whether good or bad, must come to pass in the person's life. This explains why the Bible advises us to guard our hearts with all diligence.

Keep thy heart with all diligence; for out of it are the issues of life.

— Proverbs 4:23

The passage above says we should keep our hearts with all diligence because the issues of life come from the heart. Every issue of life emanates from the heart. Getting married is an issue of life; enjoying your marriage is an issue of life; financial prosperity and good health are also issues of life. Everything you can achieve on earth is an issue of life and they all emanate from the heart. This explains why we are warned to guard our hearts with all diligence because anything that enters the heart must happen. In order to guard our hearts properly, God gave us a tool to use.

The Tool For Guarding Our Hearts

The tool God gave us for guarding our hearts is the **mind**. The mind acts as a security checkpoint for the heart. The mind does not allow any information to get to the heart without first processing and accepting it. The mind is the faculty of reasoning of man.

Any information that a man receives goes into his mind first. When the mind of a person receives particular information, it reasons the information to know whether to accept it or not. When the mind accepts the information, it will feed belief to the heart, and the heart will believe the information. So, the heart believes the information because the mind has accepted it. If a person's mind refuses to accept particular information, it will feed unbelief to the heart. So, the heart wouldn't believe the information because the mind has refused to accept it. It is the mind that determines whether the heart will believe or not. **What the mind accepts is what the heart will believe. And what the heart believes is what happens in a person's life.**

For instance, if Esther is yet to be married and I decree that she would encounter her right spouse in two hours. The information will first get to her mind to be processed. Her mind will begin to imagine how possible it is to encounter her spouse in just two hours. Her mind may also consider the efforts she had made in the past to encounter her right spouse without success. And for these reasons, her mind may not accept it.

Because her mind didn't accept that she could encounter her right spouse in two hours, then she wouldn't believe it. At the end of the two hours, she wouldn't encounter her right spouse and then she would say, "I knew it". Without knowing that she didn't encounter her right spouse within the two hours because she didn't believe it is possible. If she had believed, she would have encountered her right spouse within the two hours.

You are in charge. Your environment is controlled by what you believe. Whatever you believe in your heart is what happens in your life. And the determinant of what a person believes is the mind.

Why The Devil Focuses On The Mind

The devil knows that no one has been given power over a man apart from the man himself, and that he does not have the power to make a man fail. **He knows that whatever a person believes must happen. And he also knows that the mind is the determining factor of what a person believes. For this reason, the devil constantly attempts to corrupt the minds of people with his tricks.** If he succeeds in corrupting a person's mind, then the person would believe a negative thing. And the negative thing would then happen in the person's life.

In other words, the devil uses tricks to make people fail themselves. The devil focuses on corrupting the minds of people to make them accept failure. Once a person's mind accepts failure, his heart would believe he would fail. Anyone that believes he would fail would unfailingly fail because whatever a person believes must happen.

Spiritual Warfare Is A Game Of The Mind

Spiritual Warfare is a game of the mind. This is the reason the Bible says that the renewal of your mind leads to your transformation in life.

*And be not conformed to this world: but **be ye transformed by the renewing of your mind**, that ye may prove what is that good, and acceptable, and perfect, will of God.*
– Romans 12:2

Transformation can be defined as a change in a person, which takes him to a better level in life. A poor person becoming rich is an example of transformation. Another good example is a single person getting married. So, what the Scripture means is that for a person to experience transformation in his life, his mind has to be renewed. For you to achieve what you have not achieved before in life, your mind has to be renewed. It is a game of the mind.

Decide To Have Your Miracle Now!

Decide now to have your desired miracle. All you are required to do if you want to receive your miracle is to change your thoughts and put on the armour of God. No power is strong enough to stop you from receiving your miracle.

Do you know that the woman with the issue of blood did not pray before getting her healing? The woman suffered so much. For twelve years she had heavy daily bleeding. She really suffered. She went to various medical doctors. And I believe she went to various witch doctors. The Bible says she lost all her savings. I also believe she must have fasted and prayed so much and still did not get her miracle because Jews pray a lot. The Bible records they even pray on the street.

She eventually heard of Jesus and practised what I am teaching in this book. She did not speak to anyone and she did not pray. Her miracle started from a thought in her mind. What was her thought? That if she touches Jesus' garment she would be made whole. She then applied the most important weapon of Spiritual Warfare, which is faith. She believed her thought and when she touched Jesus' garment, she was made whole instantly.

> *When she heard about Jesus, she came up behind him in the crowd and touched his cloak,*
> *Because she **thought**, "If I just touch his clothes, I will be healed".*
> *Immediately her bleeding stopped and she felt in her body that she was freed from her suffering.*
> *– Mark 5:27-29, NIV*

The moment she touched Jesus' garment, the fountain of her blood dried up. She got her healing very cheaply. Take note that every miracle of God is cheap. If it is not cheap, it is not from God. People struggle because they don't use the weapons of our warfare. Anytime you use the weapons of our warfare, you receive your heart desires very cheaply. This explains why the woman with the issue of blood got her healing immediately she used the most important weapon of our warfare – faith.

For over twelve years, she searched for a miracle of healing without success. But when she used the weapons of our warfare, she got her miracle of healing very cheaply. The only annoying thing is that she didn't learn on time that her thought determines what happens in her life. If she had learnt it earlier, she wouldn't have lost all her savings. But that's okay. The most important thing is that she eventually got her healing.

I don't know the kind of miracle you are expecting from God. I don't know how long you have waited for it. The woman with the issue of blood waited for twelve years and still got her own. No matter what you need from God or how long you have waited for it, I declare unto you that you will receive it now in Jesus name. If the woman with the issue of blood received her miracle, then you will receive yours in Jesus name. All you need to do is to change your thought pattern.

When the woman with the issue of blood got her healing, Jesus Christ told her that her faith had made her whole. Take note that Jesus didn't say "I have healed you" He also didn't say "God has healed you" He said to the woman "*Your faith hath made thee whole*" (Mark 5:34). In other words, she was made whole because she believed her thought. I want you to know that the power you need to achieve anything in life is in you. Decide to have your miracle now and nothing can stop you.

Because the essence of this book is to empower you to achieve your heart desires, the book will not be complete if I don't expose some of the tricks of the devil. The devil uses so many tricks in Spiritual Warfare, but in the subsequent chapters, I will expose his commonly used tricks.

CHAPTER SEVEN

The Trick Of Dreams

The trick of dreams is one of the greatest tricks the devil uses to corrupt the minds of people. For a better understanding of the trick of dreams, I deem it necessary to first explain the meaning of dream and the different sources of dreams.

What Is A Dream?

A dream is a series of mental images and emotions that occur during sleep. Some can also have dreams while awake. Every dream takes place in the mind.

Sources Of Dreams

It is not every dream that comes from God. We have three sources of dreams: God, the devil and a person's thoughts.

The First Source of Dreams

The first source of dreams is God. God can put images and emotions in a person's mind when he is sleeping. Presently, we are in the dispensation of the Holy Spirit. And the Holy Spirit's responsibility, the Bible says, is to teach us all things (John 14:26) and guide us into all truths (John 16:13). Though we are not in the dispensation of dreams, God still speaks to some through dreams. A dream from God is called a revelation.

How do you know a dream from God? A dream from God must be in accordance with the Scripture. He cannot give you a revelation that is contrary to His Word. What does His Word say concerning you?

For I know the thoughts that I think toward you, saith the LORD, thoughts of peace, and not of evil, to give you an expected end.
— Jeremiah 29:11

Every dream from God is a dream of peace and not of evil. God says in the passage above that His thoughts toward you are not evil. Why then should He give you an evil dream? Any dream that makes you afraid is not from God because fear is a spirit, and it is an evil spirit. The spirit of fear does not come from God (2 Timothy 1:7). No evil dream comes from God. Every dream from God is good — a dream of peace.

The Second Source of Dreams

The second source of dreams is the devil. The devil can make a person dream. A dream from the devil is not a revelation. Dreams from the devil are always contrary to the Scripture and they are also referred to as evil dreams. The devil uses dreams as tricks in Spiritual Warfare.

The Third Source of Dreams

The third source of dreams is one's own thoughts. If you think about a particular thing and it is impressed in your mind, you can dream about it while sleeping.

How The Devil Uses Dreams As Weapon

The devil uses the trick of dreams as one of his major weapons in corrupting people's minds. Because Spiritual Warfare is a game of the mind and dreams take place in the mind, he uses dreams as a major weapon of Spiritual Warfare.

The devil uses dreams to make a person believe he has a problem so that the problem can manifest in his life. Don't forget that whatever a person believes must happen in his life. And what determines what a person believes is what his mind accepts. So the devil attempts to corrupt a person's mind by giving him an evil dream to make him believe there is a problem.

Once the person's mind is corrupted and he accepts there is a problem, then the problem will manifest.

A sister who came to my office for counselling said to me "Pastor, I had a revelation where I was tied in a dream. Please pray for me to be untied." It really amused me. First, her dream was not a revelation because it wasn't consistent with the Word of God. It is the responsibility of God to protect us in battles because His Word says that the battle belongs to Him (2 Chronicles 20:15).

Was God telling the sister He couldn't protect her and wanted her to protect herself by showing her the dream? No! It wasn't God that showed her the dream. It is God's responsibility to protect her and He doesn't have to tell her before protecting her. That dream was from the devil.

What was the essence of the dream? The devil wanted her to believe that she was in bondage so that bondage would manifest in her life. For her to be looking for a pastor to pray for her to be untied is an indication she believed she was in bondage. And because she believed she was in bondage, bondage began to manifest in her life. It is whatever a person believes that happens in his or her life.

Anytime the sister prayed to free herself from the bondage, it was an indication she believed she was in bondage. And because whatever a person believes happens in his or her life, her situation worsened. So the more she prayed to free herself, the deeper she went into the bondage.

I saw the sister and there was no rope tied around her. The rope was tied in her mind. What would set her free from such bondage is not prayer but her realisation that she is not in any bondage. Once she knows that she is not in bondage, she would become free immediately. This explains why the Bible says that when *you know the truth, the truth shall make you free* (John 8:32).

Who can tie a daughter of Zion? Which rope will be used to tie her? Who will manufacture the rope? And who will do the tying? No one can put a child of the Most High God in bondage. Every child of God is already free and cannot lose his or her freedom. Anyone the Lord has set free is free indeed (John 8:36).

Another sister once said to me during a counselling session, "Pastor, anytime I dream of eating, I lose a major breakthrough in my life". Now, I will tell you why such things were happening to the sister so that it wouldn't happen to you. The devil had succeeded in corrupting her mind to make her believe that anytime she eats in the dream, she would lose a major miracle. She had already accepted and believed it completely with her heart.

So, anytime she was about having a major breakthrough in her life, the devil would make her dream of eating just a little food. Because she had already believed that she would lose a major breakthrough anytime she eats in the dream, she would then lose the breakthrough after eating in the dream. Whatever a person believes is what happens in his or her life.

Does Eating In The Dream Signify Spiritual Attack?

No! Eating in the dream does not signify spiritual attack. If eating in the dream means spiritual attack, the Bible would have told us. The Bible is complete. There is nothing missing in the Bible. The Scripture says that the Word of God is flawless (Proverbs 30:5, NIV). There is no place the Bible says that eating in the dream is spiritually wrong. What is in the Bible is where Apostle Peter was asked in a dream to kill some animals and eat. But Peter refused eating and called the animals common. And God detested Peter's refusal to eat in the dream. He even cautioned Peter never to call what he created common.

And he became very hungry and would have eaten: but while they made ready, he fell into a trance,
And saw heaven opened, and a certain vessel descending unto him, as it had been a great sheet knit at the four corners, and let down to the earth:
Wherein were all manner of fourfooted beasts of the earth, and wild beasts, and creeping things, and fowls of the air.

And there came a voice spake unto him, Rise, Peter; kill, and eat.

But Peter said, Not so, Lord; for I have never eaten any thing that is common or unclean.

And the voice spake unto him again the second time, What God hath cleansed, that call not thou common.

– Acts 10:10-15

If eating in the dream affects a person negatively, God wouldn't have used it to give Peter a revelation. **You should understand that no kind of food can harm us, whether in the dream or in reality.** The Bible says that even when we eat poison, it will not harm us (Mark 16:18). Eating in the dream does not signify spiritual attack.

Why Do People Eat In The Dream?

If a person goes to sleep hungry, he may dream of eating. Before Peter dreamt of food, the Bible records he was very hungry. Not hungry but very hungry.

*And he became **very hungry** and would have eaten: but while they made ready, he fell into a trance.*

– Acts 10:10

If Peter weren't hungry, God wouldn't have used food to give him a revelation. Anytime a person goes to sleep hungry, he may dream of food. This explains why many people dream of food when they are fasting.

Another reason a person can dream of food is when the thought of food is in the person's mind. A person thinking of his favourite food can dream about the food. For example, a person that is always thinking of meat would always be dreaming of meat. Before telling you the solution to the trick of dreams, let me show you how to know a dream from the devil.

How To Know A Dream From The Devil

The Scripture is the only parameter you can use in differentiating a dream from God and a dream from the devil. Every dream of God is consistent with the Scripture and dreams from the devil are not consistent with the Scripture.

The Scripture, for example, says that no weapon fashioned against you shall prevail.

> *No weapon that is formed against thee shall prosper.*
> — Isaiah 54:17

The passage above is not a prayer point. It is a statement of fact. It means that any weapon fashioned against a child of the Most High God will not prosper. The implication is that any dream where a weapon prospers against a child of God is not from God. Such dreams come from the devil. He uses such dreams as tricks in corrupting the minds of people. Dreams from the devil are not consistent with the Scripture.

The Solution To The Trick Of Dreams

You should be in charge of your dreams. Don't allow your dreams to control you. Control your dreams. No matter what you dream about, don't bother yourself. If you don't like the dream, don't meditate on it, don't ponder on it, and don't imagine it. The essence of the trick of dreams is to make a person's thoughts dwell on it. The more a person thinks or meditates on a dream, the more it becomes a reality. Whenever the thoughts of a dream you don't like come to you, bring it into captivity to the obedience of Christ (2 Corinthians 10:5). Subject your thoughts to be in accordance with the Scripture.

When you wake up after a bad dream, you can speak thus "I disallow this dream from happening in real life". It is simple. The Bible says that whatsoever you disallow on earth is disallowed in heaven (Matthew 16:19). You don't need to bother yourself praying against the dream because nothing happened. When a person is busy praying against an evil dream it is an indication he believes something bad has happened or will happen. And don't forget that whatever a person believes is what happens in his life. If you like a dream, you can speak thus "I allow you to come to pass in real life in Jesus name". Because the Bible says that whatsoever you allow on earth is allowed in heaven (Matthew 16:19), the good dream will come to pass in your life.

Don't allow your dreams to control you. Ensure you control your dreams. **Believe your good dreams and refuse your bad dreams. Unfortunately, what most people do is to believe bad dreams and refuse good dreams.** When some people dream of buying an expensive car or building a mansion, they don't believe it. Rather, they see it as a symptom of malaria fever. They feel that they had such dreams because of the malaria fever in them. But when such people dream of disappointment in their lives, they believe it and will seriously pray against it. Praying against it means they believe something bad has actually happened. And because they believe something bad has happened, the disappointment will then manifest in their lives. Many believe bad dreams and disbelieve good dreams.

A sister once came to me for counselling and said, "Pastor, I have never had a physical marriage proposal, but I am always getting married in the dream". I asked her what she does anytime she dreams of getting married. And she said she always rejects and cancels the dream because she was told that marriage in the dream means spirit husband. I asked her how she expected her dreams of marriage to manifest physically when she rejects them. The same sister would dream of disappointment in marriage and pray against it. Then when she dreams of getting married, she still prays against it. Does it mean there is no good dream of marriage? The devil is tricky. He makes people to reject good dreams and accept evil dreams.

Please ensure that you believe only good dreams and disbelieve bad dreams. Control your dreams and the devil cannot use his trick of dreams on you. Don't allow him to trick you into believing that dreams of marriage mean spirit husband/wife. In the next chapter, I will expose the trick of spirit husband/wife.

CHAPTER EIGHT

The Trick Of Spirit Husband Or Wife

This is another trick the devil uses to deceive so many people. What the devil does with this trick is to make people believe they have spirit husband or spirit wife.

What Is Spirit Husband Or Wife?

It is a doctrine that is taught mainly in some African countries. The doctrine states that demon spirits get married to human beings spiritually. And that anyone who has spirit husband or wife suffers so many afflictions, which includes disappointments, delayed marriage, separation, and divorce.

Does Spirit Husband Or Wife Exist?

Please let it be known to you that there is nothing like spirit husband or spirit wife. It does not exist. If you read the Scripture from Genesis to Revelation, there is no place where the Bible tells us about spirit husband or wife. It is annoying the way the devil has made so many people teach spirit husband/wife as sermons. Spirit husband/wife does not exist. The people that teach the doctrine of spirit husband/wife wrongly use a passage in the Bible to back up their teaching. Before explaining the passage, l would like you to read it.

And it came to pass, when men began to multiply on the face of the earth, and daughters were born unto them,
That the sons of God saw the daughters of men that they were fair; and they took them wives of all which they chose,
And the LORD said, My Spirit shall not always strive with man, for that he also is flesh: yet his days shall be an hundred and twenty years.
There were giants in the earth in those days; and also after that, when the sons of God came in unto the daughters of men, and they bare children to them, the same became mighty men which were of old, men or renown.
– Genesis 6:1-4

The passage above is what people misinterpret to believe there is spirit husband or wife. They wrongly teach that the sons of God referred to in the passage are fallen angels who had spiritual marriages with human beings. But that is wrong because verse four of the passage tells us that they gave birth to giants who became mighty and renowned men. If their children became renowned men on earth, it then means that the Bible is talking about physical marriages that took place in the physical realm. Yes, the Bible passage is talking of marriages that took place on earth and not in the spirit realm. Can marriages even take place in the spirit realm? Can spirits get married?

Do Spirits Get Married?

I want you to know that spirits cannot get married. How can a spirit get married? It is not possible. How can a being without physical body get married? It is impossible! Marriage can only be done in the physical realm and not in the spirit realm.

Some Sadducees, who believed there is no resurrection, asked Jesus Christ an interesting question. They first made reference to the Jewish Law that states that if a man dies leaving his wife behind without having an issue, then the brother should marry the man's wife to raise kids for him. And they said to Jesus Christ that a certain man from a family of seven brothers married a wife and died without any issue. The second of the seven brothers married the woman and also died without an issue. All the seven brothers married the same woman and all died without any issue. The woman also died.

Then they asked Jesus who would marry the woman at the resurrection and Jesus told them that at the resurrection, there would be no marriages because we would be like angels.

Then come unto him the Sadducees, which say there is no resurrection; and they asked him, saying,

Master, Moses wrote unto us, if a man's brother die, and leave his wife behind him, and leave no children, that his brother should take his wife, and raise up seed unto his brother.

Now there were seven brethren: and the first took a wife, and dying left no seed.

And the second took her, and died, neither left he any seed: and the third likewise.

And the seven had her, and left no seed: last of all the woman died also.

In the resurrection therefore, when they shall rise, whose wife shall she be of them? For the seven had her to wife.

And Jesus answering said unto them, Do ye not therefore err, because ye know not the Scriptures, neither the power of God?

> *For when they shall rise from the dead, they neither marry, nor are given in marriage; but are as the angels which are in heaven.*
> — Mark 12:18-25

Jesus Christ speaking in the above passage confirms that angels don't get married. Angels are spirits and they don't get married. People who teach that spirit husbands/wives exist say that they are demon spirits. Demon spirits are angels as well. They are fallen angels and they don't get married. In the Scripture, there are so many places where demon spirits are referred to as angels.

> *For if God spared not the angels that sinned, but cast them down to hell, and delivered them into chains of darkness, to be reserved unto judgment.*
> — 2 Peter 2:4

In the passage above, demon spirits are referred to as angels. Demon spirits are angels that sinned. They are angels; they are fallen angels. And Jesus Christ said that at the resurrection there would be no marriages because we would be like angels. That means angels don't get married. And demon spirits are angels. If angels don't get married and demon spirits are angels, who then are the spirit husbands/wives? **Beloved, there is nothing like**

spirit husband or wife. It is cock-and-bull story; it is complete rubbish. Spirits don't get married.

Can A Christian Have An Evil Spirit?

Spirits don't get married. But assuming they will start getting married in two weeks time, what has light got to do with darkness? (2 Corinthians 6:14) Please tell me what a demon spirit will be doing with a child of the Most High God? "What communion hath light with darkness?" the Bible asks (2 Corinthians 6:14).

Beloved it is not possible that a demon spirit can get married to a child of God. Marriage makes the couple become one. How can an evil spirit become one with a child of the Most High God? Do you know that the Bible says he that is joined unto the Lord is one spirit with Him? (1 Corinthians 6:17) If a child of God is one spirit with the Lord, how then can he or she become one with an evil spirit? How can someone that is joined with the Holy Spirit be joined with an evil spirit at the same time? Please don't be deceived by the trick of spirit husband/wife.

A Christian cannot be possessed by any kind of evil spirit. No Christian can have spirit husband/wife, serpentine spirit, marine spirit, or any kind of evil spirit. **Beloved, it is not possible for a Christian to have an evil spirit. It is impossible!** The Bible says that the body of every Christian is the temple of the Holy Spirit that lives in him (1 Corinthians 6:19). **If**

the Holy Spirit lives in the body of a Christian, will a spirit husband or serpentine spirit ask the Holy Spirit to shift so that he can enter the body of the Christian? No, it is not possible.
No one can be possessed with the Holy Spirit and an evil spirit at the same time. It is either a person is possessed with the Holy Spirit or he is possessed with an evil spirit. No one can have the two at the same time. And the Bible says that every Christian has the Holy Spirit. If every Christian has the Holy Spirit, then no Christian can have an evil spirit.

Can A Spirit Indulge In Sex?

Spirits are beings without form or shape. Spirits don't have physical bodies (Luke 24:39). This explains why evil spirits are looking for physical bodies to possess to enable them perpetuate evil. If spirits have their own physical bodies, they don't need to possess anyone before perpetuating any evil. Spirits don't have physical bodies. That means they don't have different physical body parts like heads, hands, legs or sexual organs. If they don't have sexual organs, how can they indulge in sex? Spirits don't indulge in sex.

Is There Anything Like Spirit Children?

There is nothing like spirit children. Apart from the fact that spirits don't indulge in sex, they don't have wombs and can never be pregnant. They don't give birth to other spirits. Spirits don't die (Luke 20:36) and they don't procreate. It is absurd for anyone to believe there is anything like spirit children. They don't exist. **If there is anything like spirit children, does it also mean there are spirit boys and spirit girls who grow to become spirit men and spirit women? It is total rubbish.** Never you accept such rubbish. There is nothing like spirit children, spirit husband or spirit wife.

Does Sex In The Dream Signify Spiritual Attack?

There is no place where the Scripture tells us that sex in the dream means spiritual attack. Some people teach their personal doctrines instead of teaching Scriptural doctrines. In Christianity, we ought to teach only Scriptural doctrines even when they contradict our own views. **Sex in the dream does not mean spiritual attack and it does not mean the person has spirit husband or wife.** Spirits don't have physical bodies; that means they don't have sexual organs. Because they don't have sexual organs, they cannot have sex – how much more having sex with a Christian. If sex in the dream does not mean spiritual attack, why then do some people have sex in the dream?

Why Do Some People Have Sex In The Dream?

There are various reasons why a person can have sex in the dream. I will tell you four reasons that can make a person dream of sex.

(1) The first one is abstinence from sex. When a person abstains from sex for a long time, it can make him or her think of sex and the end result is sex in the dream. Don't forget that a dream is a series of mental images or emotions that occur during sleep. Once a person's thoughts dwell on sex, he or she may dream of having sex.

(2) Another reason that can make a person dream of sex is when he/she meets someone he/she is attracted to and his/her thoughts dwell on the person. Because he/she is thinking of the person, he/she may dream of sex.

(3) When a person watching television or other media sees two people touch themselves in a manner that affects his or her emotions, he or she may dream of sex.

(4) Another reason is when a person unknowingly corrupts his/her own mind. This self-corruption of the mind usually happens during a prayer session against spirit husband/wife. When a person prays against spirit husband/wife, it is an indication that the person believes he/she has spirit husband/

wife. Such prayer corrupts the mind of the person praying. And he/she would unknowingly begin to think of spirit husband/wife and when the person goes to sleep, he/she would dream of spirit husband/wife.

So when a person prays against a spirit husband/wife, he thinks about it and subsequently dreams about it. **This is the reason most people dream of spirit husband/wife on the day they pray against it. But the day they don't pray against it, they don't dream about it because they were not thinking of it. This happens to virtually everyone that prays against spirit husband/wife.**

The Trick Of Spirit Husband/Wife Exposed

The devil uses this trick to make Christians believe they have spirit husband/ wife, marine spirit, serpentine spirit or any other evil spirit. He also uses this trick to make people believe that disappointment, delay or crisis in marriage happen to a person that has an evil spirit. And if anyone believes he or she has an evil spirit, he or she will unfailingly suffer disappointment, delay or crisis in marriage because whatever a person believes is what happens in his life.

Some people's problems actually started after hearing a teaching on spirit husband/wife. For instance, a young unmarried lady was enjoying her life until she heard a teaching about spirit husband. She was taught that anyone who dreams of sex has a spirit husband/wife. And she was also taught that a spirit husband/wife causes disappointment, delay and crisis in marriage. She accepted the teaching and it corrupted her mind. That same night, when she was sleeping, she dreamt of sex.

After having had sex in the dream, the young lady believed she had spirit husband because she was taught that anyone who dreams of sex has a spirit husband/wife. Because she believed the teaching that anyone who has spirit husband/wife would experience disappointment, delay or crisis in marriage, she started experiencing disappointments and delayed marriage.

This prompted the young lady to start attending prayer and deliverance sessions in order to cast out the spirit husband. But unknown to her, her prayer against the spirit husband indicated she believed she had a spirit husband. And because whatever a person believes happens to him or her, she began to experience more disappointments. So the more she went for prayer and deliverance sessions, the more she suffered the plight. Whereas some people who have not heard such teaching get married easily without fasting because they don't believe they have spirit husband/wife or any other evil spirit.

The devil uses the trick of spirit husband/wife to make people believe they have spirit husband/wife or any other evil spirit. And when a person believes he/she has spirit husband/wife, he/she suffers according to the teaching of spirit husband/wife because whatever a person believes happens in his/her life.

The Solution To The Trick Of Spirit Husband/Wife

The solution to the trick of spirit husband/wife is the realisation that you don't have a spirit husband/wife. Don't engage in divorcing spirit husband/wife. Praying against spirit husband/wife is not the solution. **In fact, a person divorcing a spirit husband/wife is an indication the person believes he has it. Only married people can divorce. So, such prayer makes people go deeper into the bondage because whatever a person believes happens in his life.**

What can make you free from the trick of spirit husband/wife is to know you are not married to any spirit. How can you be married and you don't know your spouse? Rather, someone else is telling you that you are married. In marriage the couple becomes one. It is not possible that you have a spouse and don't know your spouse.

Please understand that the reason people experience problems of spirit husband/wife is because they believe they have spirit husband/wife and not because they actually have it. If a sister truly has an evil spirit, it will not take more than one minute to cast out the evil spirit. Evil spirits don't argue. Once you command them to get out, they obey without any form of resistance because of who we are in Christ Jesus.

So, when a person is praying and fasting, attending deliverance sessions and doing all manner of things because he/she wants to cast out an evil spirit from his/her life, it then means there is no evil spirit in him/her. You can't cast out what does not exist! If for example you are trying to drive out a fly from a bottle that does not contain a fly, you will never succeed because there is no fly in the bottle. No matter how long you try, you will never succeed because no fly is in the bottle.

Some people have been trying to cast out spirit husband/wife from their lives for over twenty years without success. The truth is that no matter how long a person attempts to cast out spirit husband/wife from his/her life, he/she cannot succeed because spirit husband/wife does not exist.

The doctrine of spirit husband/wife is a trick of the devil. And praying to cast out spirit husband/wife is not the solution to the trick. The only solution to the trick is the realisation that you don't have a spirit husband/wife. When you know you don't have an evil spirit, you then become free. This explains why the Bible says when you know the truth; it shall make you free (John 8:32).

Never you believe you have a spirit husband/wife or any other evil spirit. Any one that believes he or she has an evil spirit suffers accordingly.

If a sister for example who desires to get married believes she has a spirit husband or serpentine spirit, then the devil has concluded his work in the sister's life and she can never get married. No matter how hard she fasts or prays, she will still experience problems like someone that has an evil spirit. In fact the more she prays against the evil spirit, the more her problem increases because praying against the evil spirit is an indication that she believes she has the evil spirit. And because she believes she has an evil spirit, she suffers like people who have evil spirits, in spite of the fact that she prays against the evil spirit. What happens to a person is what he believes and not what he prays for.

Apart from the fact that spirit husband/wife doesn't exist; no Christian can have an evil spirit. If you are a Christian, do not be deceived. You cannot have an evil spirit.

Bukky's Testimony

Bukky (not her real name) was told she had serpentine spirit and because of that, she went to various places for prayer and deliverance. In spite of the various deliverance sessions she attended, she still wasn't able to get married. No one even proposed to her. Then, in October 2007, Bukky came across our newsletter and attended a counselling session with me. On the 13th of October 2007, she attended a marriage seminar we held at the National Stadium Lagos, Nigeria and she had her marriage testimony.

"Both the teaching in the counselling session and in the marriage seminar changed a lot of things in my life. A day after the marriage seminar, on the 14th of October 2007, for the first time in my life, a man proposed marriage to me. Though I didn't accept the proposal, I was happy that for once in my life I had been proposed to. It was really amazing", said Bukky.

"Two days after the seminar, the 15th of October 2007, my cousin called me and told me she gave a Germany based Nigerian my phone number. The man later called me and we started corresponding. Few weeks later, he visited Nigeria and we met for the first time. After seeing me, he proposed marriage to me.

We got married on the 24th of March 2008 (Easter Monday). I thank God that I am married now. It is truly an amazing testimony. The first time I saw a copy of the newsletter of Covenant Singles and Married Ministries, my colleagues and I wondered if the testimonies were real because they were amazing. But now I know they are real because it has happened to me. I give God the glory", concluded Bukky.

In spite of the fact that Bukky went to various places for prayer and deliverance, it didn't change her situation. But immediately she attended a marriage seminar with me, the heavens opened over her. Why? Because she acquired the required knowledge. She realised that she doesn't have serpentine spirit. As long as she believed she had serpentine spirit, no one would ever propose to her. Who would propose to a sister with serpentine spirit? So, when she realised she doesn't have serpentine spirit, she was proposed marriage to within 24 hours. And two days after the seminar she got another marriage proposal that eventually led to her marriage in March 2008.

Beloved, if you are a Christian, then you don't have spirit husband or wife or any evil spirit. What you have is the Holy Spirit. Do not be deceived by this trick of the devil.

CHAPTER NINE

The Trick Of Curses

This is another common trick the devil uses to deceive the elect of God. The devil uses this trick to make people who are free from curses believe they have a curse in their lives. And if anyone believes there is a curse in his life, he unfailingly suffers like a cursed person because whatever a person believes happens in his life. In this chapter, I completely exposed the trick of curses. I will begin by defining a curse.

What Is A Curse?

A curse is a word enforced with supernatural powers for evil in the life of an individual, family or community. The word may be spoken, written or uttered within.

The Sources Of Curses

There are three sources of curses.

(1) The first source of curses is God.
(2) The second source of curses is the devil.
(3) The third is devil's agents like witches, occultists, and others.

It is important I state here that Christians are not permitted to curse. The Bible says bless and curse not (Romans 12:14). Jesus Christ also teaches us to bless those who curse us (Matthew 5:44). Any Christian that curses a person ceases to be a Christian automatically. Only agents of the devil are permitted to curse.

Can The Devil Curse Anyone He Desires?

The devil does not have the right to curse anyone he desires. God is fully in charge of everything happening on earth. For anyone to be cursed, God must have cursed him first. If God has not cursed a person, no one can curse that person.

> *How shall I curse, whom God hath not cursed? or how shall I defy, whom the LORD hath not defied?*
> – Numbers 23:8

No one, whether the devil or man can curse a person unless God has cursed that person. **If God has not cursed you, no one can ever curse you.**

Can Prayer Break A Curse?

If a person cannot be cursed unless God has cursed him, it means that for anyone to operate under a curse, God must have cursed him. And if God has cursed a person, do you think prayer can break the curse? No! Prayer does not break curses. There is nothing like breaking of curses. If there is nothing like breaking of curses, how then do we solve the problem of curses?

To solve any problem, it is important you first identify the cause of the problem. When you find out the cause of the problem, you have solved it ninety percent. Why do curses happen? Who owns curses? How did it originate?

The Origin Of Curses

So many people believe that curses belong to the devil but that's not true. Curses belong to God. God originated curses. The first record of a curse was when God cursed Adam and Eve (Genesis 3:16-19). So God created curses.

Why Do Curses Happen?

The reason God cursed Adam and Eve was disobedience. If disobedience was the reason the first ever curse was pronounced, then disobedience is the reason curses happen.

In the Book of Deuteronomy, God also told Moses that if anyone disobeys any of the laws, curses would manifest in the person's life (Deuteronomy 28:15-68). So disobedience is the reason curses happen.

The Solution To Curses

If disobedience is the only reason curses happen, then the only solution is obedience. Obedience is the only solution to disobedience. Prayer is important but cannot take the place of obedience.

Can anyone on earth have complete obedience? No one can have complete obedience on earth because the Bible says *there is none righteous, no, not one* (Romans 3:10). No matter how nice a person may be, no one on earth has complete obedience. And disobedience to one of the laws is disobedience to all (James 2:10).

Only one person has ever lived on earth without any form of disobedience. His name is Jesus Christ. **During the crucifixion of Jesus Christ on the Cross of Calvary, there was a divine exchange. Jesus took the form of our disobedience and gave** us his complete obedience and we were made righteous (Romans 5:19).

So, the only way to be free from any curse is for a person to give his life to Christ. Once a person gives his life to Christ, he receives the complete obedience and righteousness of Christ and becomes free from every kind of curse. It is automatic! Beloved, you have no work to do. **If before the coming of Christ, the children of God had to struggle and pray to free themselves from curses, and after the coming of Christ we still have to do some things to free ourselves from curses, then the death of Christ on the Cross of Calvary is in vain.** The only means of becoming free from curses is to give your life to Christ.

Can A Christian Operate Under A Curse?

It is not possible for a Christian to operate under a curse. People take the death of Christ on the Cross of Calvary for granted. Most people who call themselves Christians don't even believe Christ redeemed us from curses. It is very clear in the Bible that Christ has redeemed us from curses. Most people know that it is in the Bible but still don't believe it.

> *Christ hath redeemed us from the curse of the law, being made a curse for us: for it is written, Cursed is every one that hangeth on a tree.*
> *– Galatians 3:13*

The passage above says very clearly that Christ redeemed us from curses. The interesting thing about the passage is that it is in the past participle. The passage says that Christ has already redeemed us from curses. It doesn't say Christ would redeem us. It says Christ has already redeemed us.

The most annoying part of it is that some people who break curses in their lives know the passage above. And some of them even quote the passage when they are breaking curses. Some speak thus: "The Bible says that Christ has redeemed us from the curse of the law, I hereby break every curse in my life." If Christ has redeemed you, which curse are you breaking? It is very clear from the above passage that we have been redeemed from every form of curse.

Do not break any curse in your life because there is no curse operating in your life. Christ has redeemed you from curses. By anyone praying to break curses means the person believes there is a curse in his life and he will begin to suffer like someone that has a curse. If you are a Christian, do not break curses because there is no curse in your life.

Do Generational Curses Exist In Christianity?

There is nothing like a generational curse in Christianity. Generational curses exist but not in Christianity. The truth is that traits are inherited from one generation to another. Whether good traits or bad traits, they are inherited by children and can be passed on from one generation to another.

But when you give your life to Christ, your generation changes. You cease to come from the generation of your earthly parents. The Bible says you become a chosen generation (1 Peter 2:9), a new kind of generation that has never existed before. Physically, you come from the generation of your earthly parents, but spiritually every Christian is of the generation of Abraham.

Know ye therefore that they which are of faith, the same are the children of Abraham.
— Galatians 3:7

The passage above clearly says that Christians are the children of Abraham. Physically you are a child of your earthly parents but spiritually you are a child of Abraham. And don't forget that what matters most is the spiritual because the spiritual controls the physical.

You should be more concerned about the spiritual because to control the physical, you need the spiritual. And the spiritual says you are a child of Abraham. What that means is that you are no longer from the generation of your earthly parents. You are from the generation of Abraham. And if you are from the generation of Abraham, then what you inherited from Abraham is blessings because it is the trait of your father that you inherit. Abraham, your father, was blessed in all things. There was no form of curse in him. We inherited his blessings.

> *Christ hath redeemed us from the curse of the law, being made curse for us: for it is written, Cursed is every one that hangeth on a tree:*
> **That the blessing of Abraham might come on the Gentiles through Jesus Christ;** *that we might receive the promise of the Spirit through faith.*
> – Galatians 3:13-14

The Bible passage above not only says that Christ has redeemed us from curses but also tells us the reason he did so. The passage says the reason is for the blessings of Abraham to come to the gentiles through Christ. Before the death of Christ, the gentiles had no relationship with Abraham. But after the death of Christ, when a person confesses and believes that God raised Christ from the dead, he becomes a Christian. And automatically becomes a child of Abraham and inherits his blessings.

It is an insult to Jesus Christ for anyone to insinuate that a Christian can operate under a generational curse or under any kind of curse. The person unknowingly is saying that the death of Christ on the Cross of Calvary did not redeem us from curses. The person is unknowingly saying that Christ wasted his time on earth. But we know without doubt that Christ did not waste His time on earth. He successfully redeemed us from curses. No kind of curse exists in Christianity.

Why Some Suffer From Generational Curses

The reason many suffer from generational curses after becoming Christians is because they believe they are still from the generation of their earthly parents. And because whatever a person believes happens to him, anyone that believes he is from the generation of his earthly parents automatically inherits the curses in the generation of his earthly parents.

Most people who know that the Bible says we are children of Abraham are still praying to break generational curses in their lives. If you are sure you are a child of Abraham, then don't pray to break any generational curse. When a person prays to break a generational curse, it is an indication he believes he is from the generation of his earthly parents. And in that case, will unfailingly inherit the curses of his earthly parents' generation because whatever a person believes happens to him.

The Solution To Generational Curses

The solution to generational curses is the realisation that you are now from the generation of Abraham. If you are a Christian, you are no longer from the generation of your earthly parents but from the generation of Abraham (Galatians 3:7). The knowledge of this is what sets a person free from generational curse.

I must state here that prayer does not stop a person from receiving the traits of his parents' generation. Every one inherits the traits of his parents' generation, whether he prays or not. So what sets a person free from generational curses is not prayer but the knowledge that he is no longer from the generation of his earthly parents.

Once a person suffering from a generational curse realises or knows that he is no longer from the generation of his earthly parents, he becomes free from the generational curse. And he will then inherit the blessings of his spiritual father, Abraham. This is what the Bible means by saying that when you know the truth; it shall make you free (John 8:32).

Caroline's Testimony

Caroline (not her real name) came to my office for counselling in 2006. Before coming to our office, she had been to several places for prayer and deliverance without any positive result. She and her four siblings were experiencing delayed marriage. They believed they were cursed and were looking for how to break the curse. When she came to our office, I taught her the truth from the Bible.

After teaching her, I prayed for her and prophesied that she would encounter her spouse in three days time. And on the third day, as she was going to work at about 7.00 A.M., a man stopped her and proposed marriage to her. Not only did the man propose to her, he told her he wanted to marry her quickly before someone else would marry her.

Another interesting thing happened. Before Caroline could complete her marriage course in her church, all her siblings got married. So within few months, the five of them got married. These are people who have been looking for how to break curses. They thought they were operating under a curse without knowing it was the trick of the devil. You must believe that Christ succeeded in redeeming you from curses. You are not under a curse if you are a Christian.

The Trick Of Achieving Righteousness By The Law

Apart from the trick of making people who are free from curses believe they are operating under curses, there is another trick the devil uses to make people come under curses.

The devil deceives some Christians to attempt achieving righteousness by works of the law, whereas our righteousness is by grace. **The only reason we cannot operate under a curse is grace; we cannot operate under a curse because Christ**

died for us and not because we obey all the laws. So, when a person loses that grace, he or she automatically comes under a curse.

The devil deceives some people to believe they can achieve righteousness by works of the law. They want to achieve righteousness by what they eat, by what they wear or by observing the law. And anyone who relies on the works of the law for righteousness must obey all the laws before he can be righteous because disobedience to one law is disobedience to all (James 2:10). And because no one can keep all the laws without breaking one, anyone who relies on the works of the law is automatically cursed.

For as many as are of the works of the law are under the curse: for it is written, Cursed is every one that continueth not in all things which are written in the book of the law to do them.

– Galatians 3:10

The above passage says that anyone who relies on the works of the law is under a curse. The devil deceives people to rely on the works of the law so that they can come under a curse.

The Solution To The Trick Of Curses

Beloved, if you are a Christian, then you cannot be cursed. You are blessed. Don't bother yourself praying to break any curse in your life. Because if anyone prays to break a curse, it is an indication he believes there is a curse in his life. And if anyone believes there is a curse in his life, a curse will begin to manifest because whatever a person believes happens in his life. **If you don't want to be affected by the trick of curses, you must understand and believe that Christ has redeemed you from all curses.**

You should also realise that no one on earth can achieve righteousness by observing the law. **You must understand that you can only be righteous because of what Christ did and not because of what you do or what you did.** You must understand that our righteousness is a gift; it is grace. Do not rely on the works of the law.

No trick of curse can have effect on you if you don't rely on the works of the law. And as a Christian, you must realise that Christ has redeemed you from curses. You are free from all curses!

CHAPTER TEN

The Trick Of Non-Forgiveness

The trick of non-forgiveness has really affected many elects of God. The devil uses this trick to make people lose their righteousness. Before showing you how the devil uses this trick to make people lose their righteousness, let me first define the true meaning of forgiveness.

What Is Forgiveness?

Forgiveness means ignoring an act as an offence. It means a state where an act is not recognised as a sin. You have forgiven someone when you refuse to acknowledge what he did to you as an offence. When you don't recognise an act against you as a sin, then you have truly forgiven the person. For example if Felix's wife insulted him and he refuses to acknowledge the act as an offence, then he has forgiven her. Instead of being angry with her, he still showers her with love because he does not see the act as an offence. True forgiveness does not acknowledge an act as a sin.

How A Person Can Lose His Righteousness

Righteousness is a state where no sin is counted against a person; it is a state where a person's sins have been forgiven. The reason a person can be righteous on earth is not because he didn't commit any sin but because his sins have been forgiven. For a person's sins to be forgiven, there is a condition he must meet.

For if ye forgive men their trespasses, your heavenly Father will also forgive you:
But if ye forgive not men their trespasses, neither will your Father forgive your trespasses.
– Matthew 6:14-15

A person must forgive others before his sins will be forgiven. It is a condition that must be met before a person's sins can be forgiven. If a person forgives others, his own sins will be forgiven. But if he refuses to forgive others, his own sins will not be forgiven.

Even when a person who has confessed and believed that Jesus Christ is his saviour refuses to forgive, his own sins will not be forgiven. And when his sins are no longer forgiven, he ceases to be righteous because righteousness means a state where a person's sins have been forgiven. Though the person became righteous after confessing and believing Jesus Christ is his saviour, he lost his righteousness because he refused to forgive others. This way, non-forgiveness makes a person lose his righteousness.

How The Devil Uses The Trick Of Non-Forgiveness

The devil knows that he has no power over a righteous person. He also knows that if a righteous person commits sin, his sin will be forgiven; but if he fails to forgive others, his sins will no longer be forgiven and he will lose his righteousness.

So in most cases, the devil doesn't tempt Christians with any of the Ten Commandments. Rather, he manipulates someone else to offend a Christian. And the offence against the Christian may be so nasty that he would feel any action he takes is justified. But taking an action against the offender indicates non-forgiveness. And anyone who is unforgiving lose his righteousness.

The Purpose Of The Trick Of Non-Forgiveness

One of the primary reasons the devil uses the trick of non-forgiveness is to make people lose their blessings. I have to state here that the devil does not make use of his tricks for nothing. He does not use his trick on someone who has nothing to offer. He that is on the floor fears no fall; such person is already finished. For the devil to use the trick of non-forgiveness on someone, it means the person has just received a blessing from God.

If a righteous person for example receives a blessing from God, the devil would want to steal it. Though the blessing may not have manifested physically but the devil who is a spirit would have seen it already. Since the person that received the blessing is righteous, the devil cannot steal the blessing from him, as he does not have power over a righteous person. But the devil knows that if the person ceases to be righteous, he can steal the blessing from him. So he uses the trick of non-forgiveness on the person to make him lose his righteousness so that he can steal his blessing.

After losing the blessing, the person in most cases will forgive his offender and becomes righteous again. When he has another blessing coming, the devil will use the same trick of non-forgiveness on him. When he loses his righteousness, the devil will steal his blessing. This cycle can continue in the person's life for years and the person will be going round in circles.

The Solution To The Trick Of Non-Forgiveness

The only solution to the trick of non-forgiveness is to forgive always. No matter what anyone does to you, please forgive the person. In Christianity, we forgive everyone. We don't fight back (Romans 12:17). **Never you see forgiveness as the character of the weak. On the contrary it is the strong that forgives the weak.**
Because no one is perfect, you cannot stay on earth without being offended by people. Please note that the devil manipulates only people who are close to you to offend you. The reason is that you may not feel offended when someone that is not close to you does an unpleasant thing to you.
It is also important for you to note that if a person refuses to be manipulated by the devil to offend you, the devil will use someone else. If Judas Iscariot for example refused the manipulation of the devil to betray Jesus Christ, the devil would have used another person. Any time a person refuses to be used by the devil to offend you, the devil will use someone else. Knowing that the devil is behind every offence against you, ensure you forgive your offenders and move forward in life.
Whenever you are offended, it is an indication that a blessing has been released to you because the devil does not use the trick of non-forgiveness for nothing. So, you are not doing your offender a favour

by forgiving him. It is to your advantage when you forgive. Anytime you forgive an offender, the devil can no longer use the trick of non-forgiveness on you and you will unfailingly see the manifestation of God's blessing in your life without delay. **The only solution to the trick of non-forgiveness is forgiveness.**

The Mystery Of Forgiveness

Forgiveness makes a person free from the law and non-forgiveness makes a person come under the law. By a person being unforgiving, it means the person has judged and found the offender guilty. And the unforgiving person automatically comes under the law because it is the law that judges.

Whenever a person acknowledges an act as a sin, it means he has judged and condemned the other as an offender or sinner. For you to believe a person sinned against you means you have judged the person and condemned him as a sinner. **And when a person judges, he comes under the law automatically because it is the law that judges. This explains why the Bible says that anyone who judges a person judges the law and sits in judgement on it (James 4:11).** The Bible also made it very clear that we must not judge.

> *Judge not, that ye be not judged.*
> *For with what judgement ye judge, ye shall be judged: and with what measure ye mete, it shall be measured to you again.*
> – Matthew 7:1-2

When you don't recognise an act against you as a sin, it means you have not judged the person. And because you have not judged, you will not be judged. By not judging, you have not recognised the works of the law and for that reason you will not come under the law. And if anyone is not under the law, none of his acts is regarded as sin. Because where there is no law, there is no sin.

> *For where no law is, there is no transgression.*
> – Romans 4:15

When you forgive, it implies you don't recognise the works of the law. And because where there is no law, there is no sin; none of your acts can be regarded as sin. When you don't attribute sin to your offenders, it means you are not recognising the law. And for that reason the sins you commit will no longer be imputed against you because where there is no law, sin is not imputed against a person.

> *But sin is not imputed when there is no law.*
> – Romans 5:13

Because you don't recognise a person's act against you as sin, your own sin is not counted against you. And that makes you righteous.

So the mystery of forgiveness is that if you don't recognise the works of the law by forgiving your offenders, then you will not be under the law and you will be justified freely by grace (Romans 3:24).

How To Know If You Have Forgiven Others

Forgiveness is in the heart. Most times people say they have forgiven others while they still bear grudges in their hearts. Whether you tell your offender you have forgiven him or not, what matters most is the state of your heart. Though I have realised that sometimes when people tell their offenders they have forgiven them, it helps the people to truly forgive.

The devil makes some people who have truly forgiven to feel they have not forgiven by reminding them of the offence committed against them. If you are always reminded of an offence against you, all you should do is to continually pray for the offender. The more you pray for the offender, the more you like him or her. And as you continue praying for the offender, you will have no more grudges against him or her. When you truly forgive, nothing can stop you from receiving your heart desires. We record so many amazing testimonies in the lives of our counselees who truly forgive. Read this amazing testimony of Theresa (not her real name).

Theresa's Testimony

"I want to thank the Lord for His faithfulness and for His grace upon His servant, Pastor Chris Ojigbani. In the year 2000, I went into my first ever relationship in life with a man I love. Five years later, in the year 2005, the man broke the relationship. We were supposed to get married in 2005, but my fiancé's parents refused. Their reason was that I am from a different tribe. I pleaded with my fiancé to talk to his mother, but it didn't work out. His family members were against the marriage not because there was something wrong with me but because of my tribe. My fiancé's aunty was the only one in support of the marriage. But when she couldn't convince the others, she encouraged me to forget about him and carry on with my life.

I was heartbroken and bitter. It affected my whole life. One year later, in 2006, I saw a flyer of Covenant Singles and Married Ministries and I went for a counselling session with Pastor Chris Ojigbani. During the counselling session, I was surprised that Pastor Chris focused his teaching on forgiveness. At the end of the teaching session, I decided to forgive my former fiancé and his family members.

When I left Pastor Chris' office, I summoned courage to call my former fiancé on the phone and told him I have truly forgiven him. He was happy and I was also relieved. Three days after forgiving my former fiancé, a bank executive proposed marriage to me. I was so surprised that I went back to see Pastor Chris to share the good news with him. Few days before I would have given the bank executive my consent, I got a call from my former fiancé asking for forgiveness and also asking me to marry him. I refused, but he continued pleading and told me his mother has given her consent to our marriage. He also told me why his mother gave her consent.

After he broke our relationship, his mother got a lady from their tribe to marry him. It then happened that the lady was a student of a university in the town where my former fiancé's mother lived alone. So, the lady was asked to move in with my former fiancé's mother. From the very day she moved into the house, she began to maltreat my former fiancé's mother. She sent her on errands and spoke to her rudely. My former fiancé's mother was virtually serving the lady. But because she brought the lady herself, she didn't know how to tell anybody. She kept it to herself and was going through misery until the day I called my former fiancé to tell him I had forgiven him.

After I called my former fiancé and told him I had forgiven him. It happened that his mother was in his house on a visit. So, after speaking with me on the phone, he was discussing our telephone conversation with his brother when their mother overheard them and asked what they were talking about. And he told her I called to say I had forgiven him. At that point, she broke down, began to cry and told them how the other lady had been maltreating her. She begged my former fiancé to plead with me and marry me rather than the other lady. This was why my former fiancé called to plead with me.

I refused to marry him, but his aunty, the only member of his family who supported our marriage, pleaded with me. Because I love him, I later accepted to marry him. And in April 2007, we got married. Praise God."

CHAPTER ELEVEN

The Trick Of Deliverance

This is another major trick the devil uses. He makes some people believe that Christ did not succeed in delivering them; so, they are busy looking for deliverance.

What Is Deliverance?

The Greek rendering of the word 'deliverance' is *aphesis and* it means redemption from sin; it means to be set at liberty. Deliverance means the act of being set free from the power of darkness. It means delivering a person from the kingdom of darkness and bringing him to the Kingdom of Jesus Christ (Colossians 1:13).

The reason man came under the power of darkness was sin. So when a person is redeemed from sin, he becomes free from the power of darkness. When someone is redeemed from sin, then he has been delivered. Deliverance means redemption from sin.

Who Needs Deliverance?

The whole essence of deliverance is redeeming someone from sin. It is about sin. When God created Adam and Eve, they did not have any need for deliverance because there was no sin in man. It was sin that made man go into bondage. Sin made man to come under the power of darkness and for that reason man required deliverance. What that means is that anyone with sin needs deliverance. Without sin in man, there wouldn't be any need for deliverance. So the person that requires deliverance is a person with sin.

Who Can Deliver A Person?

If anyone with sin needs deliverance, then a man who commits sin cannot deliver a person. It takes a man who does not commit sin to deliver a person who commits sin. Is there anyone on earth who does not commit sin? No, there is no one on earth who does not commit sin.

As it is written, There is none righteous, no, not one:
There is none that seeketh after God.

> *They are all gone out of the way, they are together become unprofitable; there is none that doeth good, no not one.*
> —Romans 3:10-12

The above Scripture confirms that no one can stay on earth without committing sin. **If no one can live on earth without committing sin and nobody that commits sin can deliver a person, it then means that no one on earth can deliver a person. No man can deliver (redeem) another man.**

If man could deliver man, God wouldn't have sacrificed His only begotten son in order to deliver us. He probably would have asked Prophet Elijah to deliver man; after all he was a prayerful man. Or he would have asked John the Baptist to deliver us. After all he was beheaded. Though John's head was cut off, it was not enough to deliver man.

Our deliverance (redemption from sin) cost God the blood of Jesus Christ – the only one who has ever lived on earth without committing sin and the only one who will ever live on earth without committing sin. He was not conceived of man, and did not inherit the sin of Adam. He also stayed on earth without committing sin. Because He did not inherit the sin of Adam and did not commit any sin, He delivered us successfully. And because He is the only one that will ever live on earth without committing sin, He is the only one who can deliver.

No one else can deliver a person. This explains why the Bible says only Jesus can save.

Neither is there salvation in any other: for there is none other name under heaven given among men, whereby we must be saved.
— Acts 4:12

The passage says that salvation is not in any other person apart from Jesus. Salvation means the same thing as deliverance. This means that no man can deliver another. No pastor can deliver anybody. Only Jesus can deliver. If a pastor asks you to come for deliverance, ask him if what Christ did on the Cross of Calvary didn't deliver you. Christ succeeded in delivering us. But assuming Christ did not succeed, is it a pastor that will now succeed? **Only Jesus Christ can deliver a person.**

How To Get Deliverance

Deliverance, which means redemption from sin, can only be gotten from Jesus Christ (Acts 4:12) because He is the only one who will ever live on earth without committing sin. His obedience was complete and the Bible says that we are made righteous through his obedience (Romans 5:19).

When Jesus Christ died on the Cross of Calvary, there was a divine exchange. Jesus took our sins and in exchange gave us His righteousness (1 Peter

2:24). If a person confesses and believes that God raised Jesus Christ from the dead, he automatically receives the righteousness of Jesus Christ.

That if thou shalt confess with thy mouth the Lord Jesus, and shalt believe in thine heart that God hath raised him from the dead, thou shalt be saved.
For with the heart man believeth unto righteousness; and with the mouth confession is made unto salvation.
— Romans 10:9-10

Anyone who confesses and believes that God raised Jesus Christ from the dead receives the righteousness of Jesus Christ. When a person receives Christ's righteousness, then there is no more sin found in him. When there is no more sin found in him, it means he has received redemption from sin, which is the same thing as deliverance.

So, once anyone confesses and believes that God raised Jesus Christ from the dead, he automatically receives deliverance. It is automatic!

Who Is A Christian?

When a person confesses and believes that God raised Jesus Christ from the dead, he receives the righteousness of Christ and is automatically redeemed from sin. Because he has received redemption of sin, which is also the same thing as receiving deliverance, then he becomes a Christian.

It is important to note that a Christian has already been translated to the Kingdom of Jesus Christ (Colossians 1:13). A Christian is not seeking to become a member of the Kingdom of Jesus Christ. He is already a member of the Kingdom of Jesus Christ. A Christian has been raised with Christ and is seated in heavenly places (Ephesians 2:6).

Does A Christian Need Deliverance?

How on earth can a Christian need deliverance? Christians don't need deliverance. The reason is very simple. Before a person can become a Christian, he must first confess and believe that God raised Jesus Christ from the dead. After a person confesses and believes that God raised Christ from the dead, he receives the righteousness of Christ, which makes him free from sin. Because he has been redeemed from sin, he has received deliverance. Deliverance means the same thing as redemption from sin. After the person is redeemed from sin, he then becomes a Christian.

You don't become a Christian before being delivered. For a person to become a Christian, he has to be delivered first. It is the deliverance (redemption from sin) a person receives that qualifies him to be a Christian. So, a Christian no longer requires deliverance because he has

already been delivered. It is the deliverance a Christian received that made him a Christian.
A Christian has been translated to the Kingdom of Jesus Christ (Colossians 1:13). How can a member of the Kingdom of Jesus Christ require deliverance? How can a person who has been raised with Jesus Christ and who is seated in the heavenly places (Ephesians 2:6), require deliverance? A Christian does not require deliverance.

The Trick Of Deliverance Exposed

The devil has deceived so many Christians to believe they need deliverance. Because of ignorance, many people who are already delivered are busy searching for deliverance. This explains why the Bible says *my people perish for lack of knowledge* (Hosea 4:6). Anyone that believes he is in bondage suffers like someone in bondage because whatever a person believes happens to him.

The devil also deceives some who accept they have been delivered to believe they need more deliverance. Please note that we don't have small deliverance or big deliverance. There is nothing like deliverance raised to the power 2 or deliverance raised to the power 4. Deliverance is deliverance. This explains why Jesus Christ said that whosoever He sets free is free indeed (John 8:36). Do not be deceived; once you confess and believe God raised Jesus Christ from the dead, you are delivered.

Does A Christian Need Deliverance When He Commits Sin?

The devil deceives so many people to believe that a Christian needs to undergo deliverance sessions when he commits sin. Because many misinterpret deliverance as prayer sessions, they wrongly believe that a Christian who commits sin needs to go for prayer and deliverance sessions.

Very many don't realise the import of the death and resurrection of Christ and are still living their lives as if Christ didn't come. Because such people don't understand that the death and the resurrection of Christ settled our deliverance once and for all, they wrongly believe that a Christian needs to undergo deliverance sessions when he commits sin.

Before the coming of Jesus Christ, once every year, the high priest would offer sacrifices of calves and goats for the remission of his sins and the sins of the people (Hebrews 9:7). After offering sacrifices for their sins in a particular year, he would offer another sacrifice the following year for the sins they committed that year. So once every year, the high priest offered sacrifices for their sins. But the body of Jesus Christ was offered to sanctify us once and for all (Hebrews 10:10).

The offering of Jesus Christ is not just for sins committed in a particular year. The Bible says that the offering of Christ is for the remission of our sins forever (Hebrews 10:12). So, a Christian no longer requires deliverance if he commits sin. **The offering of Jesus has taken care of our sins forever.** Through the offering of Jesus Christ, we are justified freely by grace (Romans 3:24). **Do we then continue sinning because we are under grace? No, God forbid (Romans 6:15). As a Christian, you are dead to sin and must not serve sin any longer.** But it is important that the devil doesn't deceive you to believe you are in bondage because of a sin you committed.

Never you forget you are under grace if you are a Christian. The understanding that you are under grace will make you righteousness conscious rather than being sin conscious. And being righteousness conscious does not make a person to continue in sin. Rather, it helps a person to stop committing sin.

For example, if you are putting on immaculate white clothes and you are conscious of it, you wouldn't want to sit on a chair without ensuring it is clean. Because you are conscious you are putting on immaculate white clothes, you wouldn't want it stained. When you are righteousness conscious, you don't want to lose the righteousness and for that reason you don't want to commit sin anymore. And if you mistakenly commit sin, you would feel so much guilt that next time you wouldn't want to commit the sin again.

Don't be afraid of the devil because of a sin you committed. The death of Christ already took

care of our sins forever (Hebrews 10:12). You don't require deliverance every time you commit sin. All you need to do is to confess your sin and God will completely forgive you (1 John 1:9).

Is There Anything Like Family Deliverance?

There is nothing like family deliverance in Christianity. **When you become a Christian, your nationality changes; you become a member of the commonwealth of Israel** (Ephesians 2:12). When you become a Christian, your family also changes and you become a member of the family of Abraham.

Know ye therefore that they which are of faith, the same are the children of Abraham.
— Galatians 3:7

If you are a Christian, you are a child of Abraham. Physically, you are still from your earthly family, but spiritually, you are a member of the family of Abraham. And because the spiritual determines the physical, the spiritual is more important.

Because you are from the family of Abraham, you no longer need to take people to pray at your family house because you are no longer from that family. Anyone that takes people to pray at his family house is unknowingly accepting he is from that family and anything that happens to

people from that family will happen to him. What sets a person free from any family affliction is not prayers but the knowledge that he is not from that family. This explains why the Bible says when you know the truth; it shall make you free (John 8:32). The death of Christ on the Cross of Calvary perfected everything in our lives (Hebrews 10:14). **If a Christian suffers any affliction because of what his father or grandfather did, then the death of Christ is in vain.** The death of Christ on the Cross of Calvary is not in vain; it perfected everything in our lives. In Christianity, there is nothing like family deliverance.

Does Prayer Lead To Deliverance?

Many people wrongly believe that prayer can lead to deliverance. For you to understand that prayer does not lead to deliverance, I will briefly define prayer and also define deliverance.

Prayer is communication with God. And deliverance means redemption from sin. How can communication with God (prayer) lead to a person's redemption from sin? It is not possible. **Redemption from sin, which is deliverance, can only be obtained by a person confessing and believing that God raised Jesus Christ from the dead.**

That if thou shalt confess with thy mouth the Lord Jesus, and shalt believe in thine heart that God hath raised him from the dead, thou shalt be saved.

For with the heart man believeth unto righteousness; and with the mouth confession is made unto salvation.

– Romans 10:9-10

Once a person confesses and believes that God raised Jesus Christ from the dead, he receives the righteousness of Christ. The righteousness of Christ in the person is what leads to the redemption of his sin, which is deliverance. **So, what leads to deliverance is the confession and belief that God raised Jesus Christ from the dead. And confessing and believing that God raised Jesus Christ from the dead is not prayer (communication with God).**

Prayer, which means communication with God is very good but does not lead to deliverance. **If prayer leads to deliverance, God wouldn't have killed His only son in order to deliver us. He would have directed us to pray very hard in order to obtain redemption. If prayer or works can lead to deliverance, then the death of Christ on the Cross of Calvary is in vain.**

If our redemption in Christ Jesus were not complete, we would have needed prayer to improve deliverance. But our redemption in Christ Jesus, which is deliverance, is perfect and complete. And anything that is perfect does not need to be improved on. Your fasting cannot make it better; your prayers cannot make it better. There is nothing you can do to make it better. A perfect thing cannot be better than it is and our deliverance in Christ Jesus is perfect.

Some people misinterpret our Lord's Prayer as containing prayer for deliverance because of the phrase 'deliver us from evil'.

And it came to pass, that, as he was praying in a certain place, when he ceased, one of his disciples said unto him, Lord, teach us to pray, as John also taught his disciples.

And he said unto them, When ye pray, say, Our Father which art in heaven, Hallowed be thy name. Thy kingdom come. Thy will be done, as in heaven, so in earth.

Give us day by day our daily bread.

And forgive us our sins; for we also forgive every one that is indebted to us. And lead us not into temptation; ***but deliver us from evil.***

– Luke 11:1-4

The phrase ***deliver us from evil*** does not mean deliverance. Deliverance means redemption from sin while ***deliver us from evil*** means to ***rescue us from evil influence***. The Greek rendering of the word 'evil' in the above passage is ***poneros***, *which* means evil influence like error, sexual sin, mischief or wrongdoing. Though Christians already have deliverance, the devil attempts to influence error, sexual sin, mischief, malice, wickedness or wrongdoing and many others in our lives.

So in the Lord's Prayer, Jesus taught us to ask God to lead us not into temptation, but to deliver us from evil. It means that we should ask God not to lead us to evil influence, but to deliver us from evil influence. It does not mean deliverance from the kingdom of darkness to the Kingdom of Jesus Christ. It does not mean redemption from sins. It does not mean deliverance. Prayer does not lead to deliverance.

Does A Person Experiencing Lack Need Deliverance?

When a Christian experiences delay or lack in any area of his life, it does not indicate he needs deliverance. Being a Christian does not guarantee your receiving all your heart desires. Though God does not want a Christian to experience lack, being a Christian does not guarantee your receiving all your heart desires. Despite the fact that a Christian is already delivered, it does not guarantee he will receive his heart desires. The purpose of deliverance is not for us to receive our heart desires. **The primary purpose of Christ redeeming us from sin, which is deliverance, is for us to have eternal life.**

For God so loved the world, that he gave his only begotten Son, that whosoever believeth in him should not perish, but have everlasting life.

– John 3:16

When you are delivered, rather than perishing, you will have eternal life. But for you to receive your heart desires, you need to win your Spiritual Warfare. The natural world we live in is subject to the spiritual. The spiritual governs the natural. For you to have your heart desires in the natural, you have to win your warfare in the spiritual. Anyone who wins his Spiritual Warfare, whether the person is delivered or not, receives his heart desires. And anyone who loses his Spiritual Warfare experiences lack, whether he is delivered or not.

This explains why many non-Christians, whom you are sure need deliverance, are rich. And there are so many people you are sure need deliverance but they get married easily and even enjoy their marriages. That a person experiences lack in an area of his life does not indicate he requires deliverance. Receiving your heart desires on earth is not determined by deliverance. What determines how and when a person can receive his heart desires is his ability to win his Spiritual Warfare, which is a game of the mind. Read this interesting true-life story of Phyna (not her real name).

Phyna's Testimony

"When my mother gave birth to me, she dedicated me to an idol and since then I have never slept without being molested by demons in my dreams. Once I close my eyes to sleep, I would see myself in a thick forest where some demons fight me. Sometimes they attempt strangling me and sometimes they rape me. Anytime I close my eyes to sleep, I would struggle until I wake up. I was not even thinking of marriage. All I wanted was to have a normal sleep, even if it's for ten minutes. All my life, I had never had a ten-minute peaceful sleep.

I had gone to several places for deliverance and the problem persisted. I lost hope and wanted to commit suicide. My mother told me to come back to the village and make some sacrifices to the idol before I could become free. I refused because I am a Christian." Said Phyna.

This was the story of Phyna that prompted her to come to our office for a counselling session with me. Just when she was about committing suicide, she met a friend of hers who directed her to our ministry.

When Phyna came to our office, I taught her the true meaning of Spiritual Warfare and how to wage the war properly. And few days later, she had this testimony to give.

"When I got to Covenant Singles and Married Ministries' Office, I expected the Pastor to gather us together for prayers but he began to teach us the Bible" said Phyna "After the teaching session, I felt light and joyful. And when I slept that night, for the first time in 30 years, I slept without any molestation. It is amazing because Pastor Chris Ojigbani had not even prayed for me; he only taught me some Scriptures. When I told my brother in the morning, he said I should observe few more nights in order to be sure the molestations have stopped. Lo and behold, it has truly stopped because it never happened again. Two days after the teaching session, I also got my own accommodation, and on the third day, I got a better job.

Some people say that no one has ever-proposed marriage to them. But my own case was that men were not speaking to me. They saw me as a man. But seven days after the teaching session with Pastor Chris, a brother called me on the phone and proposed marriage to me. I was so surprised that I asked him to repeat what he said. And he did. It's amazing!"

Yes, it's simply amazing. Though Phyna attended prayer and deliverance sessions in several places, she wasn't set free from the afflictions in her life. But when I taught her the true meaning of Spiritual Warfare and she waged the warfare properly, she became free from the afflictions. The moment she learnt the truth, the molestations in her dream stopped, she got an accommodation, got a better job and received the first ever marriage proposal in her life. This explains why the Bible says that when you know the truth, it will make you free. (John 8:32)

Do not be deceived; if you are a Christian, you have been delivered. If you are experiencing delay or lack in any area of your life, you don't need deliverance. What you need is to understand the true meaning of Spiritual Warfare and wage the warfare properly. And you will in turn receive your desires.

CHAPTER TWELVE

The Trick Of Sexual Sins

The devil uses this trick to steal blessings from people. In this chapter, I will define the meaning of sexual sin and also show how the devil uses the trick on Christians.

What Is Sexual Sin?

Sexual sin can be defined as any sexual act between two people who are not married to each other. Before the coming of Jesus Christ, sexual sins were limited to physical contact, but Jesus Christ changed it.

But I say unto you, That whosoever looketh on a woman to lust after her hath committed adultery with her already in his heart.
– Matthew 5:28

In the above passage, Jesus explained that anyone who looks at another lustfully has committed sexual sin. If lustful looking means sexual sin, then kissing is sexual sin because kissing involves lustful looking. It also means that smooching is sexual sin because it involves lustful looking. Masturbation is sexual sin as well, because no one can masturbate without lusting. Other forms of sexual sins include lesbianism, homosexuality, adultery, and sex between two singles.

The Implication Of Sexual Sins

Whenever a Christian indulges in sexual sin, he ceases to be a Christian immediately. The Bible says that the body of every Christian is the temple of the Holy Spirit that lives in him.

What! Know ye not that your body is the temple of the Holy Ghost which is in you, which ye have of God, and ye are not your own?
– 1 Corinthians 6:19

The Holy Spirit lives in the body of every Christian. And sexual sins are committed with the body, which is the temple of the Holy Spirit. So, when a person commits sexual sin, the Holy Spirit departs from the person. In his prayer after committing sexual sin with Bath-sheba, David pleaded with

God to refrain from taking away the Holy Spirit from him.

Cast me not away from thy presence; and **take not thy holy spirit from me.**
— Psalm 51:11

For David to plead with God to refrain from taking away the Holy Spirit from him after committing sexual sin is an indication that the Holy Spirit departs from anyone who indulges in sexual sin. And whenever the Holy Spirit departs from a person, he ceases to be a Christian automatically.

Now if any man have not the Spirit of Christ, he is none of his.
— Romans 8:9

If anyone does not have the Holy Spirit, which is the Spirit of Christ, he ceases to be a Christian. The implication of sexual sin is that anyone who indulges in it ceases to be a Christian.

The Trick Of Sexual Sins Exposed

The devil does not tempt a person for temptation sake. Anytime the devil tempts a person, it is because the person has a particular thing the devil is interested in. When a Christian for example receives a particular miracle, the devil wouldn't like it and would want to steal the miracle from the person. But because the devil knows he does not have power over the person unless he or she ceases to be a Christian, he then tempts the person with a sexual sin. If the person commits the sexual sin, the Holy Spirit in him or her departs and the person ceases to be a Christian. When that happens, the devil will then steal the miracle from the person. Anytime a person receives a miracle and falls into the temptation of sin, the person may lose the miracle. This explains why Jesus Christ told the impotent man he healed at the Bethesda pool that if he sins, a worse thing will come upon him.

Afterward Jesus findeth him in the temple, and said unto him, Behold, thou art made whole: sin no more, lest a worse thing come upon thee.

– John 5:14

Sexual sin is one of the sins that the devil uses in tempting people to make them lose their miracles. The truth is that if a person repents after sexual sin, God will accept the person back and the Holy Spirit will come back into the person, but it would have affected the person negatively.

Even if it took the person five minutes to repent, it is enough for the devil to strike and steal a blessing from the person, and the person may start all over again. And when the person is about receiving the miracle again, the devil will tempt him with a sexual sin again. The person falls into the temptation, commits the sexual sin and the devil steals his miracle again. And the person can go round in circles for many years because of the trick of sexual sin.

The Solution To The Trick Of Sexual Sins

The only solution to the trick of sexual sin is complete abstinence from sexual sins.

Flee fornication. Every sin that a man doeth is without the body; but he that committeth fornication sinneth against his own body.
— 1 Corinthians 6:18

The best way of abstaining from sexual sin is by avoiding a situation that can lead to sexual sin. The Bible says we should abstain from every appearance of evil (1 Thessalonians 5:22). Do not stay together in a room with someone you can have sex with. If you are a female, do not visit a man in his house. And if you must visit him, let it be in the company of someone else. If you are a man, do not visit a lady that lives alone in her house. You can meet in a public place like a restaurant, a church, or an office. Do not put yourself in a position where you may not be able to resist the temptation of sex.

It is important I state here that the reason most men are still single is that they have not seen a lady they are sure would remain faithful to them after marriage. **The only means you can make a man believe you will never have sex with another man after marrying him is by not having sex with him before marrying him.** Illicit sex is very bad. Abstain from it completely.

CHAPTER THIRTEEN

The Trick Of Testimony

The devil uses this trick as a weapon in discouraging people from testifying to the good things the Lord has done in their lives. To achieve this, the devil uses two major means. He deceives some people to be shy of testifying before a congregation. And he deceives some to believe they will lose their blessings if they testify. The devil makes such people to believe that if they testify to what the Lord has done for them, evil spirits will hear the testimony and steal the blessing from them.

That is wrong because before a person's blessing manifests physically, the devil already knows. The reason the blessing manifested was that the devil couldn't stop it. **When a person is afraid of losing his blessing, whether he testifies or not, he may lose it.** You must not be afraid of testifying to the good things God has done in your life. You cannot lose your blessing because you testified; rather your blessing is perfected when you testify.

God Wants You To Testify

Whereas the devil does not want anyone to testify to the blessings of God in his life, God wants you to testify to every good thing He does in your life. One testimony of God's blessing can activate the faith of several others and they will in turn have their own testimonies. When a person hears a testimony of how someone who passed through a situation similar to his received a blessing, his faith is activated. And he receives his own blessing.

God wants you to publish His good works in your life. David in the Book of Psalms says he will declare the wondrous works of God.

That I may publish with the voice of thanksgiving, and tell of all thy wondrous works.
― Psalm 26:7

God wants you to testify to the good things He does in your life. Testifying to the blessings of God in your life means acknowledging that God is the one who did it; that it wasn't done by your own power. Whenever you testify to the good things God has done in your life, you are giving glory to God and God in turn perfects the blessing.

Testifying Perfects Blessings

Whenever a person returns to the place of encounter with God to testify to God's blessing in his life, God in turn perfects his blessing. Please take note that it is not just the testifying to a blessing that leads to the perfection of the blessing, but returning to the place of encounter with God to testify. Jesus Christ healed ten lepers and only one came back to testify, and his healing was perfected.

And one of them, when he saw that he was healed, turned back, and with a loud voice glorified God.
And fell down on his face at his feet, giving him thanks: and he was a Samaritan.
And Jesus answering said, Were there not ten cleansed? But where are the nine?
There are not found that returned to give glory to God, save this stranger.
And he said unto him, Arise, go thy way: thy faith hath made thee whole.
– Luke 17:15-19

After Jesus Christ healed the ten lepers, only one came back to testify. Do you know that the other nine were testifying about their healing? Yes, they were testifying because people who knew them as lepers would see they were healed and would ask them how they got their healing. And they would say

Jesus healed them. By telling people Jesus healed them means they were testifying. Though they were testifying to their healing, Jesus Christ was bothered that they didn't come back to the source of the testimony to give it.

Only one came back to testify and Jesus remarked that the other nine did not come back to give glory to God. **When you return to the source of your testimony to testify, you are giving glory to God.**

Jesus also said that the leper who came back to give his testimony would be made whole. Wholeness means perfection. **Your miracle is perfected when you return to testify.** Anytime you have an encounter with God that activates a particular miracle in your life, always go back to the place of the encounter and give your testimony. **Do not allow the trick of the devil to stop you from giving your testimony. Always return to the source of your testimony to give your testimony and your blessing will be perfected.**

Conclusion

Spiritual Warfare is a game of the mind. All you need is to change your mentality and you will become qualified for a miracle. I don't know what your heart desires are. But one thing I know for sure is that if you change the way you think, you will have your heart desires. Spiritual Warfare is a game of the mind.

A certain young man was working in an insurance firm as an agent on commission. The contract he had with his firm was that he would be paid commission based on the insurance policies he sells. For over one year, he was not able to sell any insurance policy. Everyday in his office, using the telephone directory, he would call people to market insurance policies to them. Sometimes, some would give him appointment to come over to explain better but none bought any policy from him. For over one year, he did not sell even one policy.

One day, he met a multimillionaire and asked him for contacts of people who could buy insurance policy. The millionaire gave him six contacts. After getting the contacts from the millionaire, his mentality changed. He believed that because the contacts came from a respectable millionaire, the people would be interested in giving him attention and subsequently buy insurance policies from him. His expectation also became very high and he completely believed that he would succeed in selling insurance policies to the people.

He called the six people and was able to get five of them on the phone. The five people gave him appointment and they all bought insurance policies from him. He was very excited. He quickly went back to the millionaire, thanked him for the names and asked for more names. To his amazement, the millionaire gave him a copy of the telephone directory. He then told the millionaire that he had been using the same telephone directory for over one year without success. He pleaded with the millionaire to give him the kind of contacts he gave him previously. And the millionaire told him he copied the names from the same telephone directory.

The young man had been using the same telephone directory for marketing for over one year without success; because he never believed he could succeed in selling insurance policy to someone who doesn't know him, without a reference. Though he didn't believe, he was still hopeful that one day he might be fortunate to get someone who would buy from him. Because he didn't believe he could sell a policy to someone who doesn't know him, he was not able to sell even one policy.

But the day he got the referral from the millionaire, he believed that it must work because the contacts came from a millionaire. His mentality changed, and he believed he would succeed. And because whatever a man believes happens to him, he succeeded in selling the policies to the referrals.

The questions I have for you now are these: what do you believe? Do you believe you can have your heart desires? What do you think will happen within seven days from now? Do you think you can have your desires within seven days? Beloved, it is in your hands. In life you get what you believe. No matter how hard a person prays, he can only get what he believes.

A centurion came to Jesus Christ and asked him to heal his sick servant. And Jesus volunteered to accompany him to pray for his servant in his house. But the centurion refused Jesus from accompanying him to his house, saying that he wasn't worthy to receive Jesus in his house. The centurion also said to Jesus that he should speak the word without coming to his house and his servant would be healed. He explained that he is a man under authority and that he issues instructions that are obeyed. Jesus then told him it would be done as he has believed and his servant was healed immediately.

> *When Jesus heard it, he marvelled, and said to them that followed, Verily I say unto you, I have not found so great faith, no, not in Israel.*
>
> *And Jesus said unto the centurion, Go thy way; and as thou hast believed, so be it done unto thee. And his servant was healed in the selfsame hour.*
>
> – Matthew 8:10,13

From the above passage, it is evident that Jesus Christ did not pray for the Centurion's servant. He did not ask God to heal the servant. All he did was to say that it should be according to the belief of the centurion, and the servant was healed at the same moment. That means that the servant was healed according to the belief of the centurion. The implication is that if the centurion didn't believe the servant could be healed, then he wouldn't have been healed. But because he believed, and Jesus said it would be according to his belief, then the servant was healed.

Everything on earth responds to belief. This is the reason most times Jesus Christ healed people, He would always say: **"And as thou hast believed, so be it done unto thee"**, **"Let it be unto you according to your faith"**, **"Your faith has made you whole"**, **"Do you believe?"** It is what you believe that happens to you and not what you pray for.

Spiritual Warfare

Prayer is very important and I encourage you to pray without ceasing. But I want you to first understand that prayer without belief does not produce result. In fact, it leads to frustration. If you want to enjoy prayer, first work on your belief, and you will be a very happy person on earth. Do you know what Jesus Christ said? He said that whatever you ask for in prayer, if you believe that you would receive it, you would have it.

Therefore I say unto you, What things soever ye desire, when ye pray, believe that ye receive them, and ye shall have them.
— Mark 11:24

Jesus Christ taught us that the only condition we need to fulfil if we want to have anything we pray for is to believe we will receive it. He said once you believe, you will receive all your heart desires on earth. **The key is belief. Whatever you believe happens to you. No wonder Jesus said that nothing shall be impossible for those that believe (Matthew 17:20).**

And the only way you can work on your belief is by renewing your mind. It is a game of the mind. When your mind is renewed, you will believe and you will then receive your heart desires accordingly. This explains why the Bible says that transformation will take place in your life when your mind is renewed (Romans 12:2). Once your mind is renewed, you would believe and subsequently receive your heart desires.

I want you to know that the devil does not have power over you, if you are a Christian. I also want you to know that God wants you to prosper in every area of your life. But if you don't believe, God cannot do anything for you. Do not blame God for any failure in your life. The power to succeed is in you and the power to fail is in you. But I advise you to choose to succeed. God also advises us to make the right choice (Deuteronomy 30:19). No one can stop you if you choose to succeed.

You have the right to decide how and when you want to have your miracle. Beloved, the choice is yours. Countless people I have taught the true meaning of Spiritual Warfare chose when to have their miracles. And they received their miracles when they wanted. So many have also chosen when to get married and they got married on their chosen dates.

Do you realise it was the woman with the issue of blood who chose when she would be healed? She did not even talk to Christ or to anyone. She just decided that she would be healed immediately she touched Jesus' garment, and the moment she touched Jesus' garment, she was healed instantly.

What are you waiting for before deciding when you want your miracle? Decide now and it will come to pass in your life in Jesus name. Do you know that I chose when to get married without having any fiancée and I got married on the day I chose? Let me briefly give my testimony.

My Testimony

In 1996, I was ready to get married but I didn't know who to get married to. I was rich but still experienced delayed marriage. I had so many ladies I could choose from, but didn't know how to go about it. At the beginning of year 2002, on the 1st of January, I decided to take my miracle of marriage by force. Though I didn't have a fiancée, I decided I would get married on my birthday, the 17th of August 2002. So, I fixed my marriage to take place on the 17th of August 2002, and I believed it. And I also believed that there was enough time to find someone and plan for the marriage to take place on August 17th.

January 2002 ended without my finding anyone I would get married to. February and March ended and I still didn't find anyone. When by June 2002, I had not found anyone; some seeds of doubt came into me. But because I believed so much I would get married on my birthday, my belief overcame the doubt.

On a Saturday, the 20th of July 2002, four weeks to my birthday something interesting happened...

Before going into full time ministry, I was a licensed FIFA Players Agent. One of my jobs as a

Spiritual Warfare

FIFA agent was to scout for soccer players in Nigeria and other African countries, and secure clubs for them in Europe. Before securing a club for anyone I would first watch the person play soccer to be sure he is good enough to play in Europe.

A female friend of mine introduced her friend's younger brother to me to secure a club for him in Europe. I decided to watch the boy play to be sure he is good enough. And on the 20th of July 2002, I took him to the training pitch of a club I use in testing my players. While the boy and I were waiting outside the field for the coach to put him in the game, I received a phone call.

The call came from an old friend. In the course of our discussion on phone, he asked me if I was married and I told him I would be getting married on the 17th of August 2002. When I told my friend over the phone I would be getting married on the 17th of August, I meant it. Though I had not found anyone to get married to, I believed so much that I would get married on that day.

The boy I took to the training pitch heard me say I would be getting married on the 17th of August and told his sister, and his sister told her friend who is also my friend. When my friend heard I would be getting married on the 17th of August, she was furious. She called me and asked why I didn't let her know I had someone I wanted to marry. I told her I hadn't found anyone to marry and she said I was a liar. She told me that her friend's brother said

I would be getting married on the 17th of August, which was four weeks from that time.

She did not believe I would be planning to get married in four weeks time and yet had not found whom to marry. Truly, I had not found anyone. I found my wife, Uche one week later; that was three weeks to the 17th of August 2002.

After proposing marriage to my Uche, she did not give me her consent until the 7th of August 2002, ten days to my birthday. I then suggested that we should get married on the 17th. When she told her parents of my suggestion to get married to her in ten days time, they felt insulted that I gave them such a short notice. Though they did not accept the ten days notice, I still did not change the 17th of August as my marriage date.

I continued confessing it in my closet that I would get married on my birthday. After Uche's family prayed about my ten days notice, they were convinced that God wanted them to allow me get married to Uche on the 17th of August. Eight days to my birthday, Uche called me and said her family had accepted we could get married on the 17th of August. And finally we got married on my birthday, the 17th of August 2002. I give all the glory to God.

I challenge you to choose when you want your own miracle. I don't know the kind of miracle you need from God. But one thing I know is that if you decide to have it now, nothing can stop you from having it. God is actually waiting for you to exercise your dominion mandate and decide when you want your miracle. Only then will God move on your behalf and will ensure your heart desires are met. **No power is strong enough to stop you from achieving any of your determined goals. No external force was given power over a man. Only an internal force can affect a man.** This explains why the devil focuses on corrupting the mind, which is an internal force. Once he corrupts a person's mind, the person would believe a negative thing and the negative thing would happen.

Because no power can stop you, all you need to do is to decide that enough is enough; decide that the fulfilment of your desires will no longer delay. I challenge you to take it by force. Do not wait any longer; take it by force now!

And from the days of John the Baptist until now the kingdom of heaven suffereth violence, and the violent take it by force.
– Matthew 11:12

If you decide that the time has come for your miracle, then your miracle will unfailingly happen. What I have taught you in this book has been tested and proven. Countless people I have taught the principle came back with amazing testimonies. If others have had their testimonies, you will also have your own amazing testimonies in Jesus name. Congratulations!

I have no doubt that you will have a testimony in few days. Do not let the trick of the devil stop you from giving your testimony. Come to our office or to any of our seminars and give your testimony. If you cannot come to our office or to any of our seminars to give your testimony, send it to us through SMS or our email. As you come back to give your testimony, your miracle will be perfected in the name of Jesus Christ. You will not lose your testimony in Jesus name.

Printed in the United States of America